D1139831

# Handbook of
## *Quilting* and *Patchwork*
## *Stitches*

# Handbook of
## *Quilting* and *Patchwork*
## *Stitches*

### The essential illustrated
### reference to over 200 stitches

## NIKKI TINKLER

Search Press

A QUARTO BOOK

Copyright © 2011 Quarto plc

Published in 2011 by Search Press Ltd
Wellwood
North Farm Road
Tunbridge Wells
Kent TN2 3DR

ISBN: 978-1-84448-679-3

Conceived, designed and produced by
Quarto Publishing plc
The Old Brewery
6 Blundell Street
London N7 9BH

QUAR.QSB

Project editor Liz Pasfield
Senior art editor Penny Cobb
Designer Karin Skånberg
Copy editor Fiona Corbridge
Illustrators Coral Mula, Carol and
    John Woodcock, Kuo Kang Chen
Photographers Paul Forrester,
    Martin Norris

Art director Moira Clinch
Publisher Paul Carslake

Colour separation by Universal Graphics
    Pte Ltd, Singapore
Printed by Midas Printing International
    Limited, China

10 9 8 7 6 5 4 3 2 1

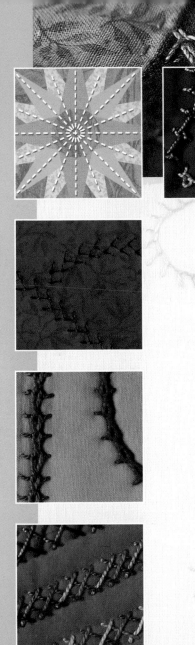

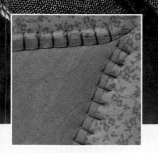
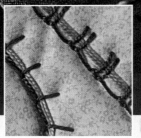

# Contents

# Introduction

Quilt-making and embroidery are two distinctly different disciplines. I am most definitely a quilter and quilt-maker, rather than an embroiderer. It is intriguing that works of embroidery are regularly exhibited within quilt exhibitions, yet we rarely see quilts and quilted work exhibited in embroidery exhibitions. I have a perennially inquisitive nature so I knew, shortly after I began quilt-making, that it wouldn't be long before I began experimenting with more exotic and textured threads, and what I now refer to as "alternative quilting stitches". It was the start of a fascinating journey.

I hope that this book opens up a whole new world of quilting for you. You may be a beginner, an embroiderer looking for a new challenge or an experienced quilter looking to expand your vocabulary of stitches; this book aims to provide inspiration and practical reference in equal measure. The keyword for this book is "experiment". So often, when we reach the

**ALTERNATIVE STITCHES**
*Hand-sewn alternative stitches can sometimes add more textural interest to quilt work than traditional stitches.*

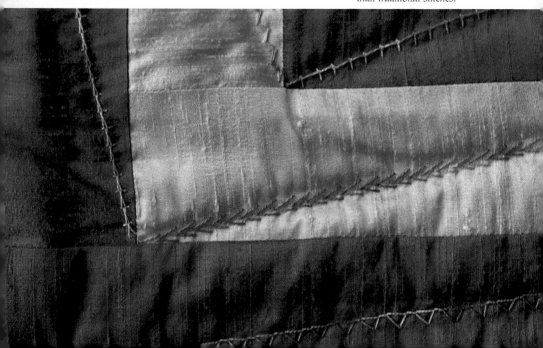

**PATCHWORK
AND QUILTING**
*Simple patchwork designs are
complemented by hand-sewn,
textural stitches.*

quilting stage of our all-important quilt projects, we
don't allow ourselves the time or the freedom to
experiment – and we've all got skeins of thread that
we've acquired, like magpies, and never touched
because we have no idea what to do with them. So, get
ready to extend your creative horizons.

## PATCHWORK

Originally, the joining of scraps of fabric to make
a patterned quilt was an attempt to make new,
yet economical, bed coverings from what had
gone before. Nothing was wasted; the
padding or wadding would often be from
another quilt or blanket, which had
become worn with age and use. For
students of textile history, the
fabrics and prints used in quilts

**ENHANCING PATCHWORK**
*Using fancy threads on traditional quilting
designs can add an extra dynamic to
basic patchwork.*

over the years are testament to the changes and constraints brought about by economic revolutions. The modern revival of interest in quilt-making has seen the practical quilt of history develop into something more sophisticated in its use of colour, fabric and design. Traditional patchwork designs are still popular, but now stunning contemporary quilts and textile art, which bring a fresh approach to the old craft, are displayed alongside them.

## QUILTING

In Europe, the practice of quilting can be traced back to Roman times, when it was used extensively for both clothing and furnishings. Early British settlers took traditional quilt-making techniques to America, where they developed into American folk art, and the quilting groups and guilds that now meet nationwide.

While there are countless forms of quilting in different countries and cultures, the basic purpose of quilting and the "quilting stitch" remain the same – to hold two or more layers of fabric together while providing some form of decoration. This can be as complicated or as simple as the quilt-maker chooses, and is open to hand-stitchers and machine-stitchers alike for exploration and experimentation.

Our ancestors, piecing patchwork quilts from old clothing and worn-out quilts, would hardly recognize a piece of contemporary textile work as a quilt, but would recognize the universal and unwavering need that quilters worldwide have to put a needle into fabric and to create patterns.

## MIXING UP STITCHES

*Contemporary quilts may contain a mixture of both machine and hand quilting. These work well together and complement the design of the patchwork.*

## STITCHES FOR QUILTING

Most people will be familiar with the traditional "quilting stitch" – that is based on the basic running stitch – but there is a lot more to quilting than just sewing a running stitch. A quilting stitch is basically a stitch that secures and holds two or more layers of fabric together; so in reality there is an enormous number of "alternative" stitches that can be used for this purpose. If a stitch is doing the job of quilting, then it can feasibly be referred to as a "quilting stitch", irrespective of its shape and size.

All the stitches in this book are based on traditional quilting and embroidery stitches. Some embroidery stitches are unsuitable for quilting because they need to be worked and remain stretched on a frame; others are not appropriate for items such as bed quilts because they are untidy on the back of the work. But many, many others can be used for quilting.

## CHOOSING STITCHES

The busier stitches offered within this book lend themselves very well to "wholecloth quilting", that is sewing a quilt that has a single piece of fabric for the quilt top, and no patchwork. Straightforward patchwork and appliquéd patterns can sometimes benefit from a little more textural interest, which can be provided by the more involved stitches. Busier patchwork and appliqué designs, however, may require the use of some of the simpler stitches. Don't forget, when quilting your designs, mix the simpler stitches, such as running stitch, chain stitch and blanket stitch, with the busier, wider and more decorative stitches, such as wheatear stitch and single-feather stitch. This will help you achieve a good visual balance within your work.

Some of the stitches will require a little more patience to perfect than others; so, perhaps if you don't like a particular stitch to begin with, at your first attempt, don't ignore it completely – have another go at a later date. You could try sewing it smaller, larger, narrower, wider, on a curve or with different thread – it may become a stitch that you come to enjoy using. All of the stitches may be sewn with finer or thicker threads than standard.

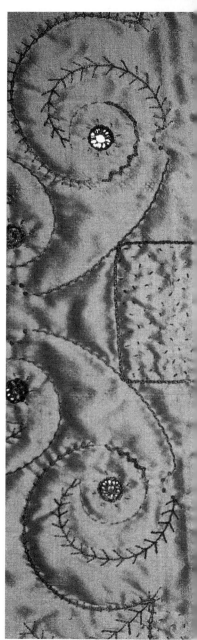

### SHOWING TEXTURE
*Textural quilting stitches are shown to their best effect on "wholecloth" quilts.*

# Quilting Essentials

Over the next few pages, you'll find suggestions for various tools and equipment that are all designed to help you make the most of your quilting and patchwork. Some of these items will already be found in your toolbox at home. Other tools and gadgets should be viewed as an investment towards your future quilt-making.

# Tools and Equipment

Specialist tools and equipment enable us to quilt to a good standard. You will already have some of the listed items; purchasing additional equipment may increase your enjoyment of quilt-making and make it less problematic.

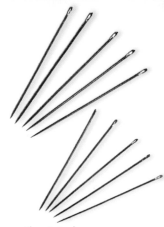

Sharps (top) and betweens (bottom)

Needles, pins and scissors are all essential; so are thimbles, a sewing machine and good lighting, depending on the techniques you prefer to use. Costs for these essentials vary enormously, but it is worth spending just that little bit more on good-quality items.

### HAND-SEWING NEEDLES

A quilting needle (known as a "between") has a short, rigid shank and a sharp point. Embroidery needles and mixed household needles can be used for the more elaborate alternative stitches and thick threads – the shank of these needles is less rigid, but the longer length is more comfortable to hold. Keep a selection of needles for the different stages of quilt construction, including tacking, hand-sewing, quilting, appliqué and beading.

### SEWING MACHINE NEEDLES

The width of a needle shank and the type of point it has (sharp or ballpoint) is designed to suit a particular weight and type of fabric. Fine needles are designed for use on delicate fabrics such as silk, voile and lawn, whereas thick needles are generally designed for fabrics of a heavier weight, such as furnishing fabrics and denim. There are special needles for jersey fabrics and leathers, and twin needles for creating a double line of stitching.

*Quilter's checklist*

Hand-sewing needles
- Embroidery needles
- Bodkin needles
- Easy-thread needles
- Beading needles
- Mixed household needles
- Betweens

Sewing machine needles
- Machine needles (different sizes for different weights of fabric)
- Twin needles
- Ballpoint needles
- Needles for stretch fabrics
- Jeans needles
- Quilting needles

Twin needles (above) and quilting needles (left), both for machine quilting

*Quilter's checklist*

**Pins**
- Bobble-headed pins
- Lace pins
- Dressmaking pins
- Safety pins
- Quilter's safety pins
- Appliqué pins
- Flathead pins

**Scissors**
- Dressmaking shears
- Serrated-edge patchwork
  scissors
- Craft scissors
- Embroidery scissors
- Pinking shears
- Appliqué scissors
- Spring-loaded scissors
- Soft-handled scissors
- Scissor sharpeners

Flathead pins

Embroidery scissors (top), left-handed scissors (middle) and craft scissors (bottom).

Bobble-headed pins

## PINS

Flathead pins are useful for keeping quilt work flat during construction. Pins with a fine shank are useful when working with delicate fabrics, but a thicker shank is more robust and suitable for use on multiple quilt layers. Lace or appliqué pins are all intended for use on fine fabrics. Bobble-headed pins are easy to handle when working with multiple layers.

## SCISSORS

It is important to invest in good, sharp dressmaking shears or serrated-edge patchwork scissors. Dressmaking shears have long blades to make it easy to cut large areas of fabric. You also need smaller scissors, such as embroidery scissors, for thread-snipping. Keep scissors for thread and fabric separate from those for paper and card. This is in order to make sure that the fabric scissors remain sharp and cut fabric cleanly without pulling at the fibres of the fabric or thread – paper and card will blunt a blade.

If you are left-handed, you may wish to purchase special left-handed scissors. The blades (and often the handle) are set differently from other scissors and consequently are more comfortable to use.

## MISCELLANEOUS NOTIONS

**Rotary cutters** should be handled with care, and always used in partnership with safety rulers and safety cutting mats.

**Quilting frames and hoops** come in a range of shapes, sizes and materials. Quilts can be clipped into lightweight plastic frames easily and quickly. Wooden floor-standing quilt frames vary from a simple round frame on a single stand to large frames designed to accommodate bed-sized quilts. For machine quilters there are quilting hoops, machine-quilting clips and "easy-grip" gloves. Seam rippers make short work of unpicking unsatisfactory stitching.

## FABRIC-MARKING TOOLS

There are countless fabric-marking tools and gadgets on the market for quilt-makers to use. However, there is no single marker that is suitable for marking every fabric, so build up a collection of different markers.

**Tools for marking fabrics** range from Hera markers, which leave an indentation on the fabric, to a variety of pens and pencils. All fabric markers should be tested

*Quilter's checklist*

Additional notions available to quilters
- Tacking gun and tacks
- Rotary cutting equipment
  (safety cutting mat, safety ruler, cutters of various sizes)
- Thimbles: metal, leather, plastic
- Bobbin boxes
- Needle-threaders
- Layout sheets
- Seam rippers
- Quilting frames/hoops
  (for hand and machine quilting)
- Hera markers
- Fabric glues
- Stencils and templates
- Cutting and pressing boards
- Tape measures
- Quilter's quarter rods
  and wheels
- Quilting gloves and quilting clips
- Lightbox
- Colour wheel
- Magnifying glass

Rotary cutting
equipment

Quilting frames
and hoops

*Quilter's checklist*

- Fabric-marking pencils for pale fabrics
- Fabric-marking pencils for dark or heavily patterned fabrics
- Fabric-marking pens for pale fabrics
- Fabric-marking pens for dark or heavily patterned fabrics
- Quilter's non-smudge lead pencil
- Fabric eraser
- Extra-long ruler
- Quilter's 6mm (¼ inch) masking tape
- Chalk wheels
- Tailor's chalk
- Large bodkin needle or Hera marker
- Air-soluble pen (vanishing pen)
- Water-soluble pen
- Dressmaker's carbon paper
- Coloured fabric-marking pens and pencils

Fabric-marking pens, pencils and eraser

Tailor's chalk

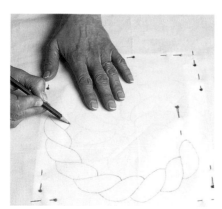

**TRACING DESIGNS**

*Quilting designs can be traced onto the quilt top before layering, while the quilt is still a single layer of fabric.*

before use to see how they react with the fabric, how well they show up and how difficult (or otherwise) they are to remove.

The list above is a good, basic selection of markers and other equipment to keep in your quilt-making toolbox.

**QUILTING STENCILS**

You may like to begin collecting specialist quilting stencils. These are available from patchwork materials suppliers and by mail order. Stencils can be used for marking designs on a quilt, either before layering, when it is a single piece of fabric, or after layering. Some stencils are described as "continuous line designs", and these allow the pattern to be stitched continuously without a lot of stop and start points, which you may prefer if you are machine quilting. Some continuous line designs are supplied as a long strip of rolled paper, which you pin or tape on the quilt top and stitch the design through the paper itself.

You may like to add quilting patterns from magazines and books to your collection. Trace the design onto the quilt top before the quilt has been layered, either by using a lightbox or by taping the design and fabric to a window (in daylight) so that the design shows through. Alternatively, trace the pattern onto a sheet of template plastic and then cut your own stencil from this.

Another way to transfer a design from a book is to trace or photocopy the design, then make holes at regular intervals along the lines of the design (either by prodding the paper by hand with a large, thick needle, or by machine-stitching along the lines

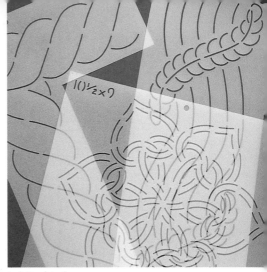

A selection of stencils

without thread in the machine (using an old, blunt needle). Once the paper has been perforated, you can transfer the design onto the quilt fabric by "pouncing" – filling a wad of cloth (an old sock or similar) with chalk and shaking it through the holes.

The tools, gadgets and techniques you choose to employ for marking a design on fabric will vary with each quilt, depending on the colours, prints and textures of the fabric used within it and whether or not the quilt has been layered. Do remember that chalks and air-soluble pens (vanishing pens) are all very temporary and useful only for short, straight lines or very small areas of quilting. If you have an elaborate design that is going to cover a large area, choose a method of marking that is easy to see and that will stay in place until the quilting has been completed.

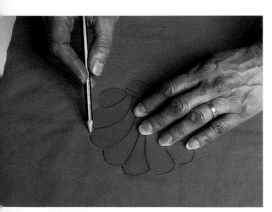

## SPECIALIST STENCILS

*Specialist quilting stencils can be used before, or after, all the quilt layers have been put together.*

# Hand-sewing Techniques

Many quilt-makers prefer to sew their work completely by hand, because they love the process of putting a needle into fabric.

Perhaps we like to get back to basics and work like our predecessors did, with a minimum of tools, equipment and expense. Whichever way you choose to sew, do remember that the making of a quilt should be viewed as a marathon and not a sprint. If you prefer hand-sewing and have the time to devote to it, don't be put off by those around you who appear to be producing machine-sewn quilts at a rate of knots. Take the time to enjoy every minute of your own work.

## PATCHWORK PIECING

When joining patches of fabric together, a small, neat running stitch with a single thread is all that is required. Mark this line with a pencil first.

At the beginning of the sewing line, use either a knot or take two or three same size stitches into the same spot ("overstitches"), so that they sit on top of each other. Begin stitching forwards along the sewing line, taking several small, neat stitches onto the needle at one time before pulling the thread through. Each time the thread is pulled through, make a small backstitch to continue the next group of running stitches; this will help to strengthen hand-sewn piecing.

Finish with several overstitches to secure the thread. Press the seams to one side, usually to the darker or busier of the two fabrics, to help to strengthen the seam and prevent any wadding "bearding" through between stitches.

**LEFT-HANDED QUILTERS**

All the diagrams in this book are aimed at right-handed quilters. If you are left-handed, most of the stitches can easily be worked as a mirror image. Stitches that are worked vertically and horizontally by right-handed quilters are also worked vertically and horizontally if you are left-handed.

When following step-by-step instructions and diagrams, try imagining that you are looking in a mirror rather than copying them exactly. Some of the diagrams will be easy to follow if they are turned upside down. When following instructions for whipped or threaded stitches, take the working thread in the opposite direction to that shown. When reading instructions, read "right" for "left" and vice versa.

## PATCHWORK ON A CURVE

*The piecing of curved seam patchwork requires careful pinning and sewing. Clip the seams gently to release any tension in the fabric.*

## APPLIQUÉ SHAPES

*Tack your appliquéd motif to your fabric before you begin to stitch.*

## STITCHES FOR APPLIQUÉ

When preparing to stitch appliquéd motifs on a background fabric, it is best to pin the appliqué in position and then use tacking thread and stitches to secure it, removing the pins as you progress.

Once the motif has been securely tacked to the fabric, there are several different stitches that can be used around the edge of it. To start the stitching, make a small, neat knot in the thread (this can be hidden inside the seam allowance of the turned-over edge of the appliqué, or even left on the reverse side of the background fabric, as this will be hidden eventually).

**Slipstitch** Use a small slipstitch to catch up a small piece of backing fabric and a small piece of the appliqué in one go, and pull the thread through. Continue in this way around the motif.

**Ladder stitch** Work a ladder stitch by catching up a small section of the background fabric with the needle, then pull the thread through and take a small section of the appliqué, directly on the folded edge, and pull the thread through once more. Make four or five ladder stitches before gently pulling the group of stitches tight.

**Blanket stitch** Work blanket stitch around the edge of the appliqué. It can be used to secure either a folded edge, or a raw edge (if bonding web has been grafted onto the back of the appliqué).

**Running stitch** Make a small, neat row of running stitches just inside the edge of the appliqué.

## MAKING UP A QUILT

There are various stages in quilt construction: making the quilt top, layering the fabrics that make up the quilt (quilt top, wadding and backing fabric), tacking the layers together, quilting and binding.

**Tacking** Use cheap thread and a fairly long needle for speedy tacking. Thread the needle with a generous length of thread. Knot the end, or work several large but fairly loose "overstitches" on the same spot.

Make large even tacking stitches, approximately 2.5 cm (1 in.) long, ensuring that all the layers of the quilt are caught up. Work several stitches in a group before pulling the thread through. Finish the line of tacking with several overstitches to secure the thread.

### Quilting with a traditional quilting stitch

Traditionally, a quilter's needle called a "between" would be used, along with a specialist quilting thread.

Cut a length of thread 30-45 cm (12-18 in.) long. Thread the needle by using the thread in the same direction as it comes off of the reel, to help to prevent knots and tangles. Make a neat knot in the end of the thread. Take the needle into the quilt top fabric and wadding only, and bring the needle up at the starting point for the quilting design.

Pull the thread through and "pop" the knot into the wadding to secure it.

Holding the needle almost perpendicular to the

**TRADITIONAL QUILTING**

*Use a quilter's between needle and specialist quilting thread for traditional hand quilting.*

**TRIMMING THE LAYERS**

*Once the quilt layers have been tacked, trim the surplus fabrics away for easier handling.*

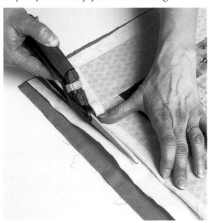

---

**REVERSE OF WORK**

If you are sewing by hand, the appearance of the stitches on the reverse of your work will not remain absolutely consistent (they are liable to vary more than on the surface of your work). Remember: these stitches are being sewn by hand. Make allowances for altering stitches, changing the position of your hands and stopping and starting to renew threads.

fabric, take the needle down and then up again in one movement, making sure that all of the layers are caught up. Take several stitches like this on the needle at a time before pulling the thread through, just tight enough for the thread to be lying on the surface of the fabric.

Continue stitching the quilting design until you have approximately 10 cm (4 in.) of thread left, or until you have reached the end of the design. Make a neat knot in the remaining thread, close to the surface of the fabric.

If you have room for one more stitch, take the needle into the top fabric and wadding only, bringing the needle out of the fabric approximately a needle's length away from the finishing point, and pop the knot into the wadding to secure it. If there is no room for an extra stitch, make a backstitch before popping the knot.

**Threaded or whipped stitches** Thread or whip the base stitch in one direction with one colour of thread, and then thread or whip the stitches a second time, in the opposite direction, using the same colour for a denser effect, or a second colour for more visual impact. A dramatic effect can be achieved by whipping or threading the base stitch with interesting yarns. The loops that are created can be left fairly loose in a decorative project such as a wallhanging or a framed work. However, if you are working on a quilt that will be laundered and handled excessively, pull them a little tighter so that they do not catch and snag.

**Working stitches in from different angles** Move the needle to a different

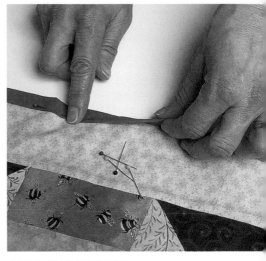

**ATTACHING BINDING**
*Slipstitch the folded edge of binding fabric neatly to the back of your quilt.*

angle, rather than trying to turn your whole hand and wrist joint at an awkward angle.

**Wide stitches** When marking out a design in preparation for quilting a project, do not draw parallel tramlines for sewing the wider stitches. Overall evenness will come naturally.

**Binding** When hand-sewing a binding fabric to a quilt, first use a backstitch so that all the layers and bulk at the edge of the quilt are strengthened.

When the binding is folded to the back of the quilt, a neat slipstitch is all that is needed to secure the fabric and cover the existing row of backstitching.

# Machine-sewing Techniques

We live in a wonderfully advanced world of technology.
Most of the sewing tasks that our predecessors spent
hours and days carrying out can now be whizzed
through in a matter of minutes with a machine.

There is an enormous array of sewing
machines to choose from. If you plan to
buy a good, basic sewing machine, it
should be light enough to lift easily,
provide basic stitches such as straight
stitch and zigzag stitch and have no
drawbacks such as temperamental
tension problems. For more
experimental work such as free-form
quilting or machine embroidery, you
ought to have a machine that also has
the facility to lower the feed dogs.

## PATCHWORK PIECING

When joining pieces of fabric by sewing
machine, cut the patches of fabric to
include a seam allowance of 6 mm
(¼ in.), then align the raw edges
alongside the 6 mm (¼ in.) foot on the
sewing machine, or put a 6 mm (¼ in.)
mark on the machine as a guide.
Alternatively, mark the sewing line
with a pencil.

Set the machine to use straight stitch.
Test both the tension and the stitch

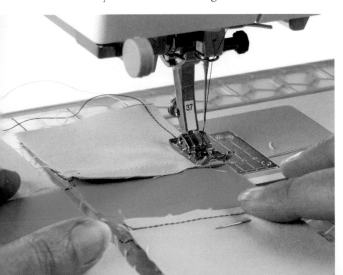

## MACHINING PATCHWORK

*Several pieces of patchwork
can be passed through the
sewing machine, one after
the other, to speed the
piecing process.*

length on a folded scrap of fabric before starting. Place a small, folded piece of scrap fabric in front of the first patch, and start your line of stitches on the scrap. Most sewing machines perform better if stitching is started in the centre of a piece of fabric rather than close to a raw edge. Stitch to the edge of the scrap fabric and then continue directly onto the edges of the patches to be joined. Continue stitching and when you reach the end, stitch directly across the seam allowance and off the raw edges of the fabric to finish. If you need to continue with more piecing, bring the line of sewing onto either another small, folded scrap of fabric, or onto the next two patches to be sewn together.

Press the seams to one side, as with hand-sewn pieced patchwork, or press them open for a flatter appearance.

## STITCHES FOR APPLIQUÉ

When preparing to stitch appliquéd motifs on a background fabric, pin the shapes in place, then secure with tacking thread and stitches, and remove the pins as you go. Pins can get in the way of the needle. Once secure there are several basic sewing machine stitches that can be used to sew around the edges or the motifs.

**Zigzag stitch** This is usually available on the most basic sewing machines. The width and length can be altered to suit the fabrics and threads used, the size and shape of the motifs and your required end result. Use on raw-edge or folded-edge appliquéd shapes.

**Satin stitch** Satin stitch is a closed-up variation on zigzag stitch and will give a heavier, denser end result. Care needs to be taken to achieve a neat finish. Particularly suitable for use on raw-edge appliqué.

**Blanket stitch** Blanket stitch can be used where a more decorative, yet open,

### MACHINE-SEWN APPLIQUÉ

*A variety of sewing machine stitches can be used to secure appliqué motifs in place. The stitch you choose will depend on how complicated your motif is and whether or not you have a raw edge of fabric to be covered.*

stitch is needed. The "spikes" of blanket stitch can either radiate outwards from the appliqué or inwards. The length and width of the stitch can be experimented with. Use on raw-edge or folded-edge appliquéd shapes.

**Straight stitch** A simple row of straight stitch can be sewn just inside the edge of the appliqué motif. Straight stitch can also be used when free-form sewing, to secure motifs. Particularly suitable for use on raw-edge appliqué.

**Overlocking stitch** This stitch can be found on more expensive sewing machines and, where a less noticeable stitch is preferred, it can be used with an invisible thread to provide a good substitute for hand-sewn appliqué. Particularly suitable for use on folded-edge appliqué.

### TACKING

Virtually every part of a quilt can be sewn on a sewing machine, including the tacking. Set the machine to use straight stitch, and set the stitch length facility to the longest available setting. (Alternatively, if your machine has it, use the tacking stitch facility.)

Machine-sewn tacking stitches will have a tighter tension than hand-sewn tacking, so make allowances so that the backing fabric is not pulled too tight by this added tension.

### MACHINE QUILTING

If you enjoy using your sewing machine, you'll probably enjoy experimenting and pushing the boundaries of machine quilting. In comparison to a hand-quilted project, machine quilting will produce a

**USING MACHINE QUILTING**
*Machine quilting, an essential part of the construction of a quilt, which secures the three layers together, should not be confused with machine embroidery, which is used primarily for embellishment.*

slightly more rigid quilt, which is also flatter in appearance. There are two distinctly different techniques used for machine quilting: straight stitching and free-form stitching.

**Straight stitch technique** Use a straight stitch, with the feed dogs in the normal position, to:
- Quilt in the ditch (literally, to sew in the valley of the patchwork seam).
- Contour-quilt around fabric patches.
- Echo quilting.
- Sew continuous line quilting designs.
  On a folded scrap of fabric, test both

the tension and the stitch setting before starting. If you have an even-feed foot (dual-feed or walking foot), fit this in place so that all layers of the quilt will pass through the machine evenly. Or place pins at right angles to the seam at regular intervals, removing them as the needle approaches.

Start sewing with the needle in the "down" position at the starting point of the design. Use the stitch-locking facility if you have this on your machine. Alternatively, lock the threads by reducing the stitch length to 0.5 and making one stitch forwards, one back, one forwards and one back. Stitch along the patchwork lines or marked quilting design, and finish the line of machine-sewn quilting in the same manner as you began.

**Free-form technique** For free-form quilting (also known as random, stipple and free-motion quilting):
• Lower the feed dogs.
• Fit a machine embroidery foot (free-form quilting foot).

Set the stitch length and stitch width settings to zero. Fit the machine with a large needle (size 100). You may also find you need to adjust the tension on your machine – work on a practice piece first to establish what is needed.

Place your quilt work within a machine-quilting frame, or use machine-quilting gloves or gripping brackets to keep a secure hold on your work. Slide the work under the needle and bring both the top thread and the bobbin thread to the surface of the work; hold these firmly away from you while you lower the presser foot.

Make two or three stitches on the

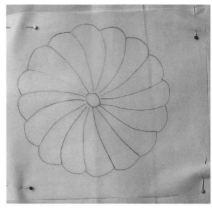

**CHOOSING DESIGNS**

*Look for designs with a continuous line when machine quilting. These have less "start and stop" junctions.*

same spot to lock the threads. Begin moving the work underneath the needle as you press down on the foot pedal, and start stitching your design.

This technique requires some practice. Remember, you are moving the fabric yourself, instead of the machine moving it with the feed dogs. Finish by making two or three stitches on the same spot to lock the threads before snipping them to neaten.

**BINDING**

When adding binding fabrics to a quilt, a straight stitch is all that is needed to begin with. This will ensure that all the layers of the quilt and binding are caught together in a strong seam.

Once the binding has been folded to the back of the quilt, a slipstitch sewn by hand can be used to cover the line of machine-sewn stitching.

# Fabrics

*Fabrics with prints*

When choosing fabrics for patchwork, try to eliminate those that are difficult to handle, or have a very open weave and are liable to fray excessively.

Two fabrics are ideal for beginners: 100 per cent cotton and "Dupion silk" (make sure they are craft or dress weight and avoid using furnishing fabrics at this stage). When starting out, you will benefit from using the same weight of fabric throughout your quilt. Once you become more confident, you can diversify and introduce more interesting or exotic fabrics. Slippery, lightweight or open-weave fabrics can always be backed with an iron-on interfacing to make them more stable, but do remember that this added layer may make the fabrics more difficult to quilt by hand.

## WASHING

Make sure that fabrics are both washable and colourfast: many patchworkers prefer to prewash all their fabrics before using them in a quilt, just to be on the safe side, but we all know how wonderful new fabric feels. If you choose to prewash fabrics before cutting into them, you can get that "new" feel back by using a spray starch at the ironing stage – this will help give some stability back to the washed fabric and

make it easier to handle and cut into.

It is possible to use old clothes and other fabrics if they have a sentimental value for you. You must be aware, though, that these fabrics will have been worn, handled and laundered far more than a new fabric and, therefore, may wear through far sooner and at different rates to new fabric.

## FABRIC COLLECTION

When building a stash of fabrics, try to achieve a good selection of prints – large, medium and small – alongside a selection of plain fabrics (or prints that are so subtle that they "read" as plain from a distance). Keep a diverse selection of colours. You may stick to navy, beige and white within your wardrobe, but a restricted colour palette in a fabric collection may restrict your creativity when it comes to patchwork. Most specialist patchwork and quilting shops sell bundles of fabric known as stash-builders; these are small pieces of fabric specifically cut and sold together to enable you to build your collection at

*Plain fabrics*

_Silks and metallics_

minimum cost. However, if you do prefer a restricted and more subtle fabric palette, don't forget to inject that all-important tiny piece of strong colour very gently, here and there, to add interest.

### COLOUR AND TONE

Tonal values are important for adding definition to patchwork patterns – you need a range of tones in each colour, from dark tones, through medium tones to light tones. A lot of people find it difficult to see the tonal values of fabrics, but here are a couple of tips. First, cut swatches of fabric in a particular colour, such as red, and lay them in a tonal strip, ranging from dark to light. Glue these to a sheet of paper and photocopy it on a black and white photocopier. Second, if you have a digital camera, set it to black and white photography mode and take a picture of the fabrics. Both methods will help you to see the tonal values more clearly than looking at the actual fabric colour itself.

Another thing to bear in mind is that the tone of one fabric may alter, depending on the fabric that is placed next to it.

### THE BACK OF A QUILT

If you choose a plain fabric for the back of a quilt, remember that the stitches will show up more clearly than if you choose a patterned fabric. If you are happy with the appearance of the stitches on the back of your quilt, it does not matter whether the backing fabric is plain or print. However, when stitching appears to be very busy or uneven on the back of your work (perhaps you have had to stitch through thick and bulky patchwork seams and junctions, for instance), a backing fabric printed with a pattern may be preferable. This is not an excuse for sloppy work, but it may just take some pressure off you at the quilting stage of a project.

_Stripes and checks_

# Threads

Many different types of thread are available for use in both quilted and embroidered projects. It's a good idea to consider the fabrics that you've used throughout a quilt before choosing the thread for the construction stages and quilting stages.

For instance, if a project is predominantly made from silk, you may prefer to carry the theme through and use a silk thread, especially where fine, hand-stitched appliqué is concerned.

If the quilt has been constructed from fairly robust 100 per cent cotton, it makes sense to continue with the natural fibre theme by using 100 per cent cotton thread for both construction and quilting.

## HAND-QUILTING THREADS

For traditional hand quilting, quilting thread is available in a whole host of colours, both as mercerized cotton and polyester fibre. There is no need to run the quilting thread through a block of beeswax before using it, as early quilters did. However, if you tend to twist the needle and thread while you are sewing, beeswax may certainly go a little way toward preventing the thread from tangling and knotting.

| HAND-QUILTING THREADS |
|---|
| 1 HAND-QUILTING THREAD: 100% cotton |
| 2 HAND-QUILTING THREAD: 100% cotton, extra strong |
| 3 HAND-QUILTING THREAD: cotton-covered polyester, extra strong |
| 4 SILK THREAD: 100% silk, very fine |
| 5 COTTON PERLE: 100% *coton à broder* – available in different weights |
| 6 COTTON PERLE: 100% cotton crochet yarn – available in different weights |
| 7 METALLIC THREAD: 100% polyester yarn – not very strong, but useful for embellishment |

### VARIEGATED/SPACE-DYED THREADS

8 PEARL COTTON: 100% cotton, twisted, glossy thread – available in different weights

9 PERLE THREAD: 100% cotton, hand-dyed

10 SASHIKO THREAD: 100% cotton, specialist thread for Sashiko quilting

Some machine-quilting threads such as 100% mercerized cotton and 100% long-staple cotton are also suitable for hand-sewing.

## MACHINE-QUILTING THREADS

1  COTTON: 100% cotton all-purpose thread, suitable for hand-sewing and machine work

2  POLYESTER: 100% polyester all-purpose thread, suitable for hand-sewing and machining

3  SILKY: 100% viscose glossy embroidery thread

4  SILKY: 100% acrylic glossy embroidery thread

5  METALLIC: 60% polyester, 40% polyester high-gloss thread

6  METALLIC: 70% polyamide, 30% polyester fibrous thread

7  METALLIC: 100% polyester high-gloss, hologram-effect thread

8  INVISIBLE THREAD: man-made fibre for "invisible" machine quilting

## VARIEGATED/SPACE-DYED THREADS

9  MACHINE QUILTING: 100% mercerized cotton

10  MACHINE QUILTING: 100% long-staple cotton, suitable for heavier quilting or topstitching

When choosing fabrics and threads for a quilt project, especially for some of the more decorative stitches, remember that it is always possible to work a large stitch with fine thread on thick and heavy fabric. It is virtually impossible to work a tiny stitch with thick thread through a fine fabric.

### MACHINE-QUILTING THREADS
When it comes to choosing machine-quilting threads, there is an enormous choice of threads designed for both machine quilting and machine embroidery.

Give some thought to the fibres that are in the materials that you've used for the quilt, and to which machine-quilting technique you will use

**Using machine-quilting thread** Before beginning to machine-stitch have a trial run on some scrap fabric layered with a length of wadding.

Test both the upper and lower tensions on the machine: one or the other may need to be adjusted, especially if you have loaded the bobbin with a thread in a different weight to that on the top of the machine. Using metallic thread often requires a slight adjustment to the tensions, as does free-form machine quilting or machine embroidery with the feed dogs lowered.

Check the stitch length, width and setting (if using a preset stitch). Finally, choose a selection of threads and try them out on your practice piece first. That way, you'll be more relaxed and confident when it comes to using the machine on your precious quilt.

# Construction Materials

The final appearance of a quilt and the ease with which it is quilted will depend very much on the "filling in your sandwich", i.e. the wadding and stabilizer fabrics.

## WADDING

The choice is wide and varied – there are waddings that are specifically designed for hand quilting, waddings that are manufactured to support machine quilting, and some that are suitable for either. There are several things to consider when choosing the wadding for a quilt project:

- The quilting technique and threads you will be using.
- The final appearance you would like your quilt to have.
- The sort of wear and tear that the quilt will be subjected to.
- Your budget.

**Techniques and threads** Some waddings designed for machine quilting are very difficult to work through if quilting by hand. If you plan to mix the two techniques within one quilt, opt for a wadding that is suitable for both hand and machine quilting, so that you get the best of both worlds.

**Final appearance** A wadding made of 100 per cent polyester will give a lot of loft (plumpness) to the puffs and pillows of a quilting design. However, it will flatten if you try to iron the quilt at a later date. Many of the waddings made from natural fibres or mixed fibres have a more compressed appearance and, therefore, the quilt will have a flatter appearance, too. This is fine for a wallhanging, but you might prefer a plumper appearance for a bed quilt, in which case it would be better to use a higher loft wadding.

**Wear and tear** If you are making a quilt for a child, or an elderly person who is living in a retirement home, it may experience a great deal more laundering than might otherwise be expected. Choose a wadding that will live up to the extremes of laundering in a washing machine at a fairly high temperature. Some waddings are preshrunk, others will have to be preshrunk by the quilter before being used. Some quilters prefer to purposely "antiquate" their quilts after they are made by using a wadding that will specifically shrink and make the quilt look older than it is.

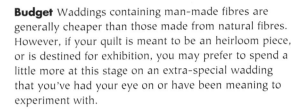

**Budget** Waddings containing man-made fibres are generally cheaper than those made from natural fibres. However, if your quilt is meant to be an heirloom piece, or is destined for exhibition, you may prefer to spend a little more at this stage on an extra-special wadding that you've had your eye on or have been meaning to experiment with.

## STABILIZERS

Stabilizing fabrics are commonly used in needlework for dressmaking and soft furnishings. Their uses in quilt-making are less well known, but when dealing with materials of different weights, different structures and varying durability (such as silks of different quality, or open-weave fabrics such as calico or cheesecloth, Indian cottons or Osnaburg), they are invaluable.

### SOME OF THE WADDINGS AVAILABLE

1 POLYESTER (FLUFFY):
High loft, easy to launder.

2 POLYESTER (COMPRESSED):
Thermal qualities.

3 POLYESTER (GREY/BLACK):
For use with dark fabrics.

4 100% COTTON:
Flatter appearance, very stretchy, may need prewashing to shrink.

5 100% COTTON WITH SCRIM:
Designed for machine quilting; may need prewashing.

6 COTTON/POLYESTER MIX:
Has the feel of natural fibres with less stretch than 100% cotton. May provide some controlled shrinkage for effect.

7 100% WOOL:
Quite expensive; extra care needs to be taken with storage and cleaning.

8 100% LAMBSWOOL:
Very dense and fluffy; expensive.

9 WOOL/POLYESTER MIX:
Less stretchy, same considerations needed for storage and cleaning as 100% wool.

10 SILK:
Very expensive, more difficult to use, a little unstable.

## STABILIZERS FOR QUILT-MAKING

1 IRON-ON INTERFACING:
   Available in different weights.
   Sew-in interfacing.

2 QUICKSCREEN INTERFACING:
   Useful as a permanent
   foundation fabric.

3 BONDING WEB:
   Used for bonding fabrics when
   doing raw-edge appliqué.
   Available in different weights. Use
   baking parchment to protect your
   iron and ironing board cover.

4 FREEZER PAPER:
   Used as a support for
   appliquéd motifs.

Other commonly used stabilizers are:
tear-away stabilizer (useful for
foundation pieced patchwork), water-
soluble interfacing (for machine
quilting/embroidery; it dissolves when
immersed in water and is available for
use in hot or cold water), heat-soluble
interfacing (it disintegrates when heat
is applied), heavyweight interfacing
(used to mould three-dimensional
shapes) and sheer gauze (for
capturing decorative threads).

**Utility materials** All of these can
provide a stabilizing effect within quilted
work used for items such as placemats,
purses and millinery, as well as quilts.
• Muslin. Available in different weights.
• Buckram.
• Canvas.
• Calico or cheesecloth.
• Insulating fabrics with thermal
  properties.

## FOUNDATION MATERIALS

5 TEMPORARY:
   Tear-away stabilizer,
   brown paper, waxed
   paper,photocopy/
   typing paper.

6 PERMANENT:
   Calico, muslin,
   quickscreen
   interfacing, fabric.

# Fabric Preparation

Fabrics must be prepared before you can begin work.

## PREWASHING FABRICS

- Prewash if you are unsure about the stability of a fabric (whether it has been preshrunk or not) and if you have any doubts about its colourfastness.
- If the quilt is to be laundered regularly, it is wise to prewash the fabrics to see how they behave in a washing machine at different temperatures. Once a fabric has been washed, it may need stretching back into shape.
- If you've prewashed fabrics and they feel flimsy, give them a new lease of life by adding spray starch when you press them. They'll feel good as new and be easier to handle.

## REASONS NOT TO PREWASH FABRICS

- There's nothing as nice as the feel of brand new fabrics; they usually contain a dressing or starch, which makes them more resistant to creasing.
- Lack of opportunity. Short, one-day workshops held within a shop usually involve using fabric straight off the shelf. In this situation, try to choose colours that won't be so prone to dye loss, and opt for good-quality printed and closely woven fabrics.
- Hand-dyed fabrics have usually been washed so many times in the dyeing process that they have no shrinkage left in them by the time they are used within a quilt. Be wary, though, of dyes that are notoriously difficult to set, such as reds and purples. Use a dye-catcher cloth in the washing machine and a cool temperature setting.

## GRAIN

- Check the grain on a fabric before cutting into it. The lengthwise grain is known as the "warp" and runs down the length of the fabric; the crosswise grain is known as the "weft" and runs across the width of the fabric between the two selvedges.
- The warp and weft are the straight grain. Where stability is needed, items should always be cut on the straight grain, especially within patchwork.
- Grain that runs diagonally across the width of the fabric (at an angle of approximately 45°) is known as the "bias". Bias-cut fabric is very stretchy: Once stretched, it won't spring back into place, so be careful where you use bias-cut edges. It is ideal for strips or patches of fabric that need to be manipulated around a curve.

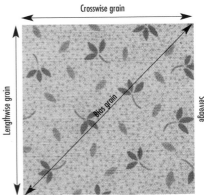

Crosswise grain

Lengthwise grain

Bias grain

Selvedge

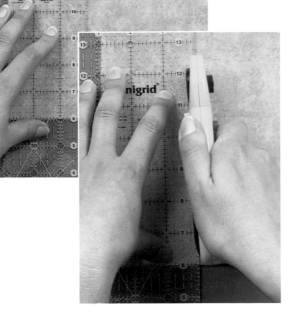

## ROTARY CUTTING

*When using a rotary cutter to cut fabric always use a specialist cutting mat, safety ruler and a sharp blade. It is safer to "bridge" the hand that is holding the ruler. Always cut away from yourself rather than towards yourself.*

## SAVING TIME

*Using spring-loaded scissors with long blades can make short work of cutting fabrics by hand.*

## CUTTING INTO FABRIC

- Before cutting into a length of fabric, remove the tightly woven selvedges so that they don't distort the main body of the material. Iron out any creases.
- If using rotary cutting equipment, large lengths of fabric can be folded to fit the cutting board. Up to eight layers of fabric can be cut into easily, but make sure you're using a sharp blade.

## MIXING FIBRES

If you're using fabrics of various fibre types within a quilt project, take the time to stabilize the weaker ones with an iron-on interfacing or calico. This will ensure that all the fabrics are easy to handle and have more or less the same weight when it comes to the quilting process. It also makes the aftercare of the quilt easier.

# Quilt Construction

Quilt construction begins with the making of the quilt top. You may have chosen to piece this in patchwork, you may have preferred stitching appliqué, perhaps you've mixed the two, or perhaps you've made a wholecloth quilt, with no piecing or embellishment at all.

Whichever methods you chose for the quilt top, once you're ready to work on the next stage – the layering – give the top a good press.

## HOW TO BEGIN

Choose, prepare and press the backing fabric. This needs to measure approximately 5–10 cm (2–4 in.) larger all around than the quilt top, to allow for any reduction in size caused at the quilting stage. Remove the selvedges to reduce any tension at the sides of the fabric.

If the quilt is large and you've chosen standard-width fabric, the backing fabric may need to be cut and joined. (It is possible to buy extra-wide fabric, which is sold specifically for backing quilts.) Press the seams open to flatten them. (If you've hand-sewn them, press the seams to one side to strengthen them.)

## BACKING FABRIC

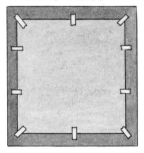

*Choose an area that is large enough for you to lay out the complete quilt; this could be a generous-sized tabletop or the floor. Lay out the backing fabric, right side down, square it up and smooth it out. Using low-tack masking tape, tape down the four corners of the fabric and, in the case of larger quilts, the halfway point on each side. This will keep the fabric flat and taut while you add the next layers.*

## WADDING

*If the wadding has been prepacked, unwrap it and spread it out on a bed or similar area to allow it to breathe, preferably overnight.*

*If the wadding is narrower than the quilt, you may have to join sections of wadding together: place two edges alongside each other, butting together neatly without overlapping, and then stitch them together with a large whip stitch or* cross stitch, a neutral thread and a big needle. Make sure that the join in the wadding is not too near to the edges of the quilt.

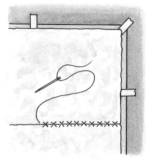

Again, the wadding needs to measure approximately 5–10 cm (2–4 in.) larger than the quilt top: make it the same size as the backing fabric if you can. When you're ready, lay the wadding on top of the backing fabric and gently tape the four corners (and the halfway points if you're working on a large quilt). Make sure any lumps have been smoothed out.

## QUILT TOP

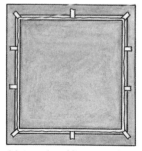

Now lay the quilt top, right side up, on top of the wadding. Ensure that the edges are parallel with the edges of the backing fabric and wadding, smooth out any ripples in the fabric and tape it in the same way. If you prefer, you can add a few pins to stop the layers from travelling while you work on them.

## TACKING

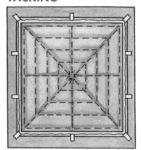

The tacking stage needs to be worked from the centre outwards: begin by tacking the cross-grid (the vertical and horizontal lines that pass through the centre) and the full diagonals. Start each line of tacking in the centre and work outwards. Follow this by working a grid all over the quilt in each direction. This can be worked from side to side, or on one quarter of the quilt at a time. Aim to work a grid of approximately 5–7.5 cm (2–3 in.) wide – this will stop the layers of the quilt from travelling when you reach the quilting stage.

## ⊙ TIP

There are alternatives to tacking in the traditional fashion: you may prefer to hold the layers together with safety pins, or use a tacking gun and clips. These are a good option if you need to work in a hurry, or you are restricted for space in which to do the tacking, or if you prefer machine quilting (sometimes a tacking thread can get caught up in machine quilting).

# Marking and Quilting

## MARKING A QUILT BEFORE LAYERING

There are various ways to carry out marking of a quilt before layering.

**Window** In daylight, tape the design to a window, tape the fabric over this and trace the pattern. This technique is only suitable for pale fabrics. See photographs opposite for other methods.

## MARKING A QUILT AFTER LAYERING

This is by far the easiest stage at which to mark a quilting design, because the quilt top fabric has been stabilized by adding further layers.

All of the fabric-marking options suggested under Fabric-marking Tools (see page 14) are available to you at this stage (except for tracing a design). If you choose to stitch your quilt in a frame or a hoop, any designs for a section will need to be marked before the work is set into the frame.

**Marking a design** Mark up the design over the entire quilt top before you start, or mark each section as you go. This may have a bearing on which marking tool or gadget you use and how long the marks have to stay put while the quilt is being handled. A powdery chalk, for instance, will soon disappear as you begin to quilt. A chemical-based pen, such as a water-soluble pen, will stay in the fabric for longer, but the marks may need to be removed as the quilting progresses if you are worried about permanent setting.

**Stencils** Use stencils and templates to add further interest. Choose designs and patterns that complement the quilt itself. Blocks of patchwork can have parts of templates/stencils stitched within patches of fabrics.

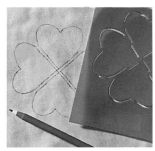

**HOME-MADE STENCIL**
*Another option is to trace the design onto template plastic and make your own stencil. Use a craft knife or a special stencil-cutting hot knife to cut out the design. If the design is linear only, make a photocopy of it, glue it to some card and cut around the outer edge of the design to make a template.*

## QUILTING STITCHING METHODS

### CONTOUR-QUILTING

Contour-quilting involves quilting around each part of a design to outline it. Quilt around individual pieces of patchwork or appliquéd motifs.

### ECHO QUILTING

This method of quilting allows you to create exciting patterns by quilting around a patch or motif and then echoing the shape of this stitching by stitching further lines that run parallel to it.

### QUILTING IN THE DITCH

Quilting in the ditch is a method of adding puffiness to a quilt with unobtrusive stitching that does not detract from the design. To do it, work a straight stitch in the dead centre of the seamline.

### INFILL STITCHING

Once appliqué motifs have been contour quilted, areas of background fabric can be quilted with infill stitching designs.

### BORDERS AND CORNERSTONES

The quilting of borders can be incorporated into the whole design, or they can be quilted separately. Long borders can provide an opportunity to use a long run of interesting designs such as cable, cable and feather, plaits or vines. Cornerstones and setting squares within quilts can provide a good canvas for interesting square patterns.

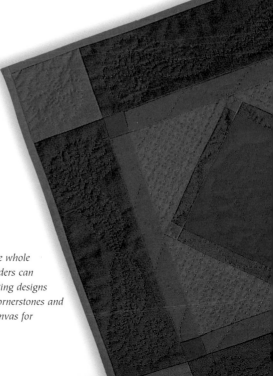

# Types of Quilting

Quilting and quilt-making are universally popular. It is fascinating to see how different countries have approached needlework in this form and how cultural influences have determined a recognizable type of quilting from each corner of the world.

# Sashiko Quilting

This form of quilting comes from ancient Japan. The most identifiable work is stitched with a thick, white perle thread and a simple running stitch through two layers of indigo-dyed cotton fabric, with no wadding between the layers. Sashiko was originally used as utility stitching on garments and later became a form of decorative "embroidery". It is simple to adapt Sashiko "embroidery" to do the job of quilting and a variety of brightly coloured Sashiko threads, preprinted stencils and patterns are available.

 **TIPS**

Sashiko designs are based on a grid, so you need squared paper when designing your own patterns. You may also like to use paper printed with an isometric grid for triangles, hexagons or diamonds, etc. Several designs may be used within a project.

**PREPRINTED DESIGNS**
*Some shops stock pads of paper printed with designs that could easily be interpreted in Sashiko quilting.*

**DESIGNS**
*Regular curvilinear and geometric designs such as these are all suitable for Sashiko quilting.*

## MARKING THE FABRIC

Mark your chosen design on the fabric. It could consist of a single all-over pattern, or of several sections, each filled with a different pattern.

## STARTING TO STITCH

Tie a neat knot in the thread: this can be "popped" through the top fabric and into the wadding, as with traditional quilting.

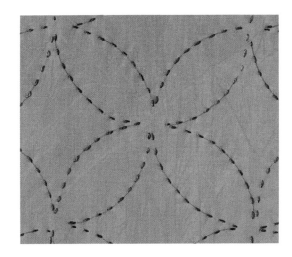

## STITCH LENGTH

In Sashiko quilting, longer stitches are traditionally sewn. Stitch your design using approximately 3–5 running stitches per 2.5 cm (1 in.).

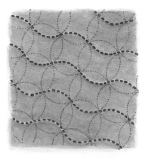

## CONTINUOUS STITCHING

Work continuous lines of stitching from one side of a project to the other. Study the design and work out how to sew as many lines as possible continuously, in order to have the fewest breaks in the thread.

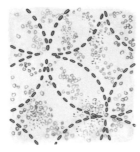

## JUNCTIONS

When several lines of a design meet at a junction, leave a space between the stitches (or at that particular junction) rather than having the stitches overlap or run into each other.

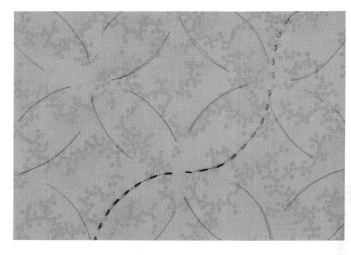

## FINISHING

Complete each line of the design by "popping" the knotted thread through the top fabric once again, into the wadding layer, and snipping the tail of thread to finish neatly.

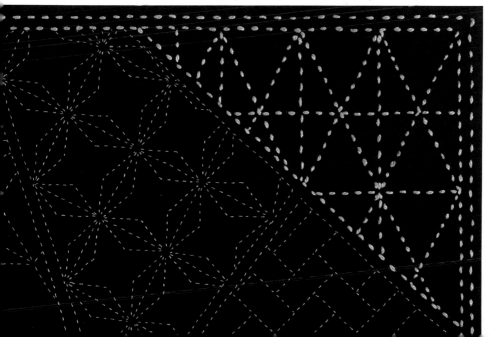

# Italian Quilting

Italian quilting has been popular throughout Europe and the Middle East for centuries, both for embellishing garments and on bed quilts. Wadding is not used. It consists of corded channels, which give an attractive three-dimensional effect. These are produced with traditional quilting wool and a large-eyed blunt needle. This technique is used mainly on wholecloth quilts. The French equivalent is called *Boutis*, and uses very fine cord to produce a more intricate design.

## DESIGN SECTION

**KNOTS**
*Knot design with suitable areas for cording.*

**HEARTS**
*Heart design with suitable channels for Italian quilting.*

 **TIP**

Choose a design that incorporates, or can be interpreted, with "tramlines" (double parallel lines). These will be the channels and should be of a size to comfortably accommodate the cording thread or wool you are using. Mark the design on the fabric.

## MATERIALS SECTION

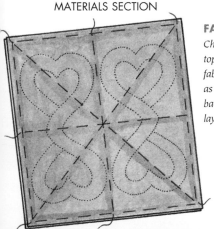

**FABRICS**
*Choose a fine cotton for the top layer. You will also need a fabric with a loose weave, such as calico or cheesecloth, to back this. Tack the two layers together.*

 **TIPS**

• Make sure the yarn that you choose for cording has been prewashed to prevent shrinkage at a later date.
• For additional interest, use coloured wools such as knitting yarns, under a top layer of fabric that is almost transparent.

## CHANNELS SECTION

**HAND-SEWN CHANNELS**
*Channels may be stitched by hand using running stitch, backstitch or chain stitch.*

**MACHINED CHANNELS**
*Channels sewn by machine require a medium-length stitch.*

**STITCHING THE BASIC DESIGN**
*Stitch the channels of the design prior to cording.*

## CORDING SECTION

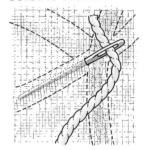

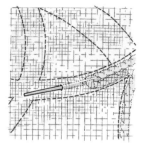

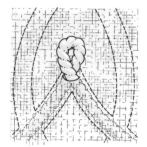

### NEEDLE

*Use a blunt tapestry needle or bodkin to run the yarn through the channels in the design. Insert it through a small slit made in the calico backing.*

### PULLING THE CORD THROUGH

*Bring the needle out of the calico backing at regular intervals.*

### TENSION LOOPS

*Leave small loops of cord on sharp curves or corners.*

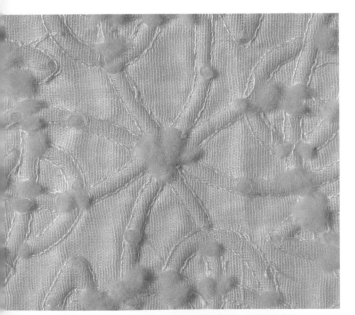

### TENSION LOOPS THROUGHOUT A DESIGN

*Loops of wool or yarn are left outside the calico on curves and corners to prevent the quilting being pulled too tight.*

---

### ◎ TIPS

• Tension loops will settle into place as the work is handled and will prevent the fabrics from being distorted by overly tight cording.

• Stop and start a new length of yarn when turning a sharp corner or at junctions in the design. Leave "stop" and "start" tails of yarn outside the calico.

## QUILTING SECTION

*A piece of Italian quilting may also be further quilted to help throw the corded design into relief. Once the entire design has been padded with yarn, layer the work with a backing fabric, or a backing fabric plus a thin, compressed wadding (so that the wadding does not detract from the corded areas).*

*Quilt around the entire design, making quilting stitches directly next to the original outline stitching.*

## CORDING AND QUILTING

*A design that has been corded with Italian quilting, and then hand quilted afterwards for added effect.*

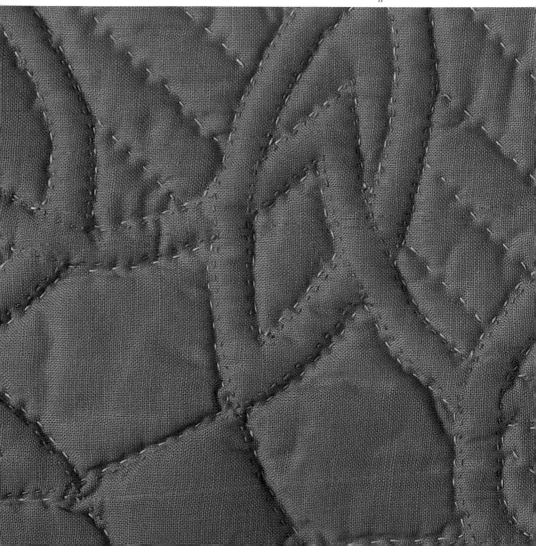

# Trapunto

Trapunto adds a dimensional effect to quilt work by the insertion of stuffing into areas of the design. It is traditionally used on wholecloth quilts (without patchwork or appliqué). Trapunto has a long history and has been used for clothing, soft furnishings and bed quilts. Although highly decorative, it is also quite time-consuming to produce. Designs are marked as for traditional quilting. A layer of calico is then placed behind the top fabric to hold the stuffing in place.

### CHOOSING THE STUFFING

*The stuffing needs to have a loose consistency. Use specialist toy stuffing or pull apart scraps of polyester wadding. You will find it easier to manipulate the stuffing if you use a pair of tweezers, especially for the smaller areas.*

### MARKING THE DESIGN

*Begin by marking the design on the fabric. Choose a design with "enclosed" areas that are ideal for being padded, such as this flower and feather.*

### APPLYING CALICO

*Add a layer of fine calico (or cheesecloth) to the reverse side of the fabric and baste the two layers together.*

### STITCHING THE DESIGN

*Using a self-coloured thread and a small, neat stitch (hand-sewing or machining), stitch along all the lines of the design. Any thread knots can be left at the back of the work as they will eventually be hidden by further layers.*

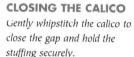

### PADDING THE DESIGN

*Determine the first area to be padded. Make a small, neat cut in the calico covering this area, not too close to the stitching lines. Using a pair of tweezers, push small scraps of stuffing behind the calico. Don't overstuff the area, as this will distort the surface fabric.*

### CLOSING THE CALICO

*Gently whipstitch the calico to close the gap and hold the stuffing securely.*

### ALTERNATIVE METHOD

*Alternatively, prise the fibres of the calico apart to form a hole large enough for the stuffing to be pushed through, and then gently manipulate them back into position to close the gap.*

## COMPLETING
## THE PADDING

*Repeat this process to pad all the relevant areas of the design.*

## ADDING A BACKING

*Layer the work, either with a backing fabric and no wadding, or a backing fabric and a light, compressed wadding (so that the stuffed areas do not become confused with unstuffed areas).*

## QUILTING THE DESIGN

*Quilt around the design, making the quilting stitches directly next to the original outline stitches of the design. Quilting the background areas will make the padded design stand out even more.*

# Kantha

Kantha quilting originated in Bangladesh, where it was often stitched on sari fabric. A small, neat running stitch is employed throughout. Coloured threads are used to sew a decorative border and to outline a central design. The design is then infilled with various colours and shapes. The coloured threads can be chosen to add areas of shading to the design. Traditionally, several layers of fine cotton material were tacked together without wadding. However, this technique can easily be adapted for use on padded quilt work.

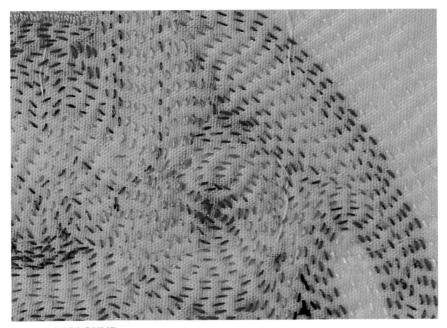

## THE BACKGROUND

*The background area around the design is filled with stitching, beginning with contour lines and echo lines around the central design itself and working outwards to fill the entire space. The background area is sewn with a thread that matches the colour of the fabric.*

## DESIGNS

*Motifs and designs suitable for Kantha quilting.*

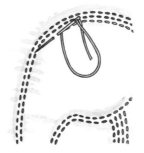

### STARTING OFF

*Make a template for the outline design and use it to mark the design on the fabric.*

### THE STITCHING PROCESS

*Begin by stitching the central design itself, using small, neat running stitches. Stitch around the outline and then fill the whole design with continuous running stitches.*

## (◎ TIPS

• Taking several stitches onto the needle at once will help with evenness, although this will be more difficult to do on tight curves.

• Use different shades of thread colour to add shadow and light to the design in a painterly way.

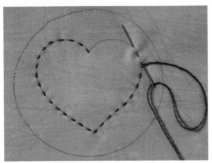

### STARTING AND FINISHING

Start your thread with a knot. "Pop" the knot through the top fabric and into the wadding or between the fabric layers to secure it.

### CENTRAL AND BORDER DESIGNS

Once the entire central design has been sewn, decide on a border design and sew this.

### QUILTING THE BACKGROUND

Take a self-coloured thread and begin contour quilting, and then echo quilting, around the central design. Continue in this way until the entire background has been filled with stitching. Finish each length of thread by "popping" the knotted thread through the top fabric and into the wadding, snipping the tail of thread to finish neatly.

# Hand and machine quilting

## KNOTTING AND TUFTING

This traditionally utilitarian form of quilting can add textural interest to a modern quilt. Thread is used to make individual knots at regular intervals through all the layers of a quilt. The tufts of thread can be sewn into the quilt layers for a neat finish, or left on the surface of the quilt top or backing fabric for effect. Buttons, charms, scraps of fabric or decorative threads can also be included.

**TYING A KNOT**
*Take the thread or yarn into the fabric layers and up again. Repeat on the same spot.*

**TUFTING**
*Leave tufts of thread on the surface of the quilt for a decorative effect.*

**EMBELLISHMENT**
*Add buttons, charms or other items as a focus of interest.*

## WHOLECLOTH QUILTING

The quilt top is made from one large piece of cloth and marked with a quilting design that covers the entire area. Patchwork and appliqué are not involved. Some designs are traditional in certain geographical locations, so it is often possible to determine where an antique quilt was made and, in some cases, help to date it.

**MARKING OUT A WHOLECLOTH DESIGN**
*Mark the quilt with a traditional quilting design that covers the whole area of the quilt top fabric, or draw a freehand and contemporary design of your choice.*

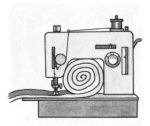

### WHOLECLOTH QUILTING BY HAND

*For hand quilting, use running stitch, backstitch or chain stitch.*

### PREPARING TO QUILT BY MACHINE

*Tack the quilt and then roll it in preparation for quilting by machine.*

### WHOLECLOTH QUILTING BY MACHINE

*Quilt from the centre outwards, working on the most difficult to reach area first and ensuring that all the quilt layers travel outwards evenly.*

### MACHINING THE DESIGN

*Try to find continuous line designs to machine, so that you don't have too many "stop and start" junctions in your work.*

### HAND-SEWN WHOLECLOTH DESIGN

*A central motif can be thrown into relief by the use of infill quilting designs in the background, such as squares, diamonds and circles.*

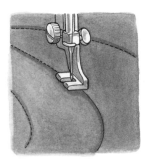

### QUILTING IN THE DITCH
This technique is used in projects where you want pieced patchwork fabrics to be more prominent than the quilting. The quilting stitches are sewn in the ditch or valley of the seam, where two pieces of patchwork have been joined together. Use an unobtrusive thread that will blend with the fabrics.

### CONTOUR- AND ECHO QUILTING
Contour-quilting can be used to emphasize areas on printed panels, printed fabrics, pieced patchwork and appliqué. Quilting stitches are sewn just to the side of the seam (or around the relevant line of the printed design).

Echo quilting is used to add definition to previous quilting and to highlight a pattern further. You can use a single echo line or several, depending on the pattern and how much of the background area you wish to fill.

### INFILL QUILTING
Infill quilting is used to add interest to an area surrounding a design that has already been quilted, and to quilt areas of background that are too large to leave unquilted. This can consist of one pattern or a combination of patterns, geometric or curvilinear, which are often designed on a grid. An infill pattern should complement the main quilted design and not detract from it.

## RANDOM QUILTING

Random designs are usually continuous and can be used to complement patchwork and appliqué, or to fill large areas such as backgrounds and borders. Although the work is not meant to follow a set design, specific patterns can be achieved, such as stipple or vermicelli patterns, geometric grids, curved lines, motifs and even lettering. All are usually sewn without premarked designs to guide the quilter. If you are unsure about this, you may prefer to draw a design to follow.

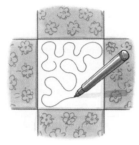

### DESIGNS

*Designs may be premarked or stitched completely randomly.*

### HAND-STITCHED RANDOM QUILTING

*Using a running stitch, take several stitches onto the needle at one time if the design allows. If your quilting pattern begins to look uniform, turn your work and head off in another direction to achieve a "random" appearance throughout the design.*

### RANDOM QUILTING BY MACHINE

*Fit a quilting foot to your machine and reduce the stitch length and width to "nil". Bring both threads to the surface of the work before you begin – you may also need to adjust your machine tension. Lower or cover the feed dogs. Your hands will be guiding and moving the fabric instead, and you'll be "drawing" with the needle.*

 **TIP**

When random quilting by machine, try using a faster stitch speed (using the foot pedal) together with a slower movement of the fabric (with your hands).

### TEXTURE AND PERSPECTIVE

*Metallic and coloured threads intermingle in this randomly quilted design. The design is stitched into sheer organza and layered over scraps of fabrics in differing greens to produce an illusion of perspective and landscape.*

# The Stitch Collection

The stitches in the following collection have been chosen for their suitability for quilting, as well as for their added textural interest.

The diagrams are crucial to the position at which you need to sew these stitches. For instance, if the step-by-step sequence shows a stitch being worked horizontally, that is because it is the easiest way to work that particular stitch. If you are tempted to turn your work and sew the stitch in another direction (for comfort, ease or preference), do turn the diagram so that it matches the way you are working and prevents confusion.

# Stitch Selector

On the next few pages you'll find all of the quilting stitches included in the book. Use this selector to choose the stitch you want, then turn to the correct page for step-by-step instructions.

STITCHES FOR HAND QUILTING PAGE 66

**PAGE 67**

**PAGE 68**

**PAGE 69**

**PAGE 70**

**PAGE 71**

**PAGE 72**

**PAGE 73**

**PAGE 74**

**PAGE 75**

**PAGE 76**

**PAGE 77**

**PAGE 78**

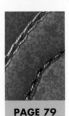
**PAGE 79**

**PAGE 80**

**PAGE 81**

**PAGE 82**

**PAGE 83**

**PAGE 84**

**PAGE 85**

**PAGE 86**

**PAGE 87**

**PAGE 88**

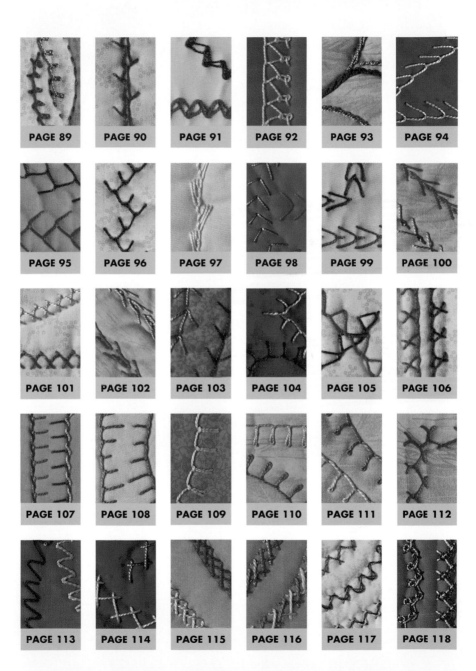

PAGE 89 | PAGE 90 | PAGE 91 | PAGE 92 | PAGE 93 | PAGE 94

PAGE 95 | PAGE 96 | PAGE 97 | PAGE 98 | PAGE 99 | PAGE 100

PAGE 101 | PAGE 102 | PAGE 103 | PAGE 104 | PAGE 105 | PAGE 106

PAGE 107 | PAGE 108 | PAGE 109 | PAGE 110 | PAGE 111 | PAGE 112

PAGE 113 | PAGE 114 | PAGE 115 | PAGE 116 | PAGE 117 | PAGE 118

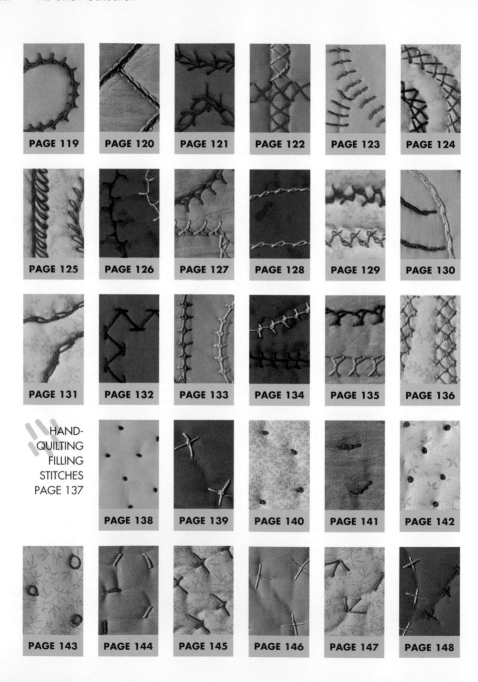

PAGE 119

PAGE 120

PAGE 121

PAGE 122

PAGE 123

PAGE 124

PAGE 125

PAGE 126

PAGE 127

PAGE 128

PAGE 129

PAGE 130

PAGE 131

PAGE 132

PAGE 133

PAGE 134

PAGE 135

PAGE 136

HAND-
QUILTING
FILLING
STITCHES
PAGE 137

PAGE 138

PAGE 139

PAGE 140

PAGE 141

PAGE 142

PAGE 143

PAGE 144

PAGE 145

PAGE 146

PAGE 147

PAGE 148

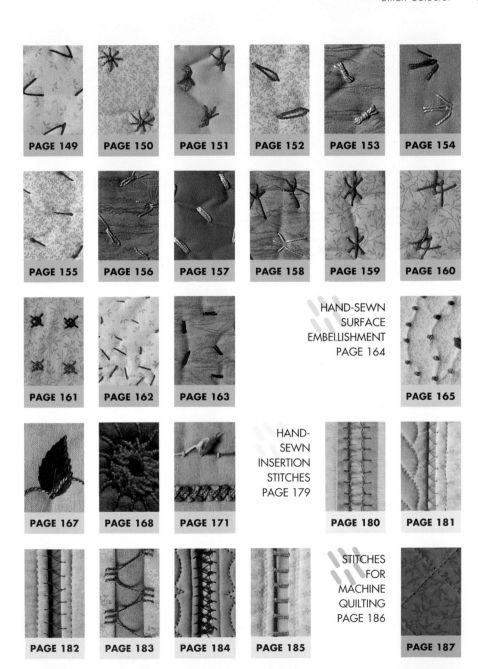

PAGE 149
PAGE 150
PAGE 151
PAGE 152
PAGE 153
PAGE 154

PAGE 155
PAGE 156
PAGE 157
PAGE 158
PAGE 159
PAGE 160

PAGE 161
PAGE 162
PAGE 163

HAND-SEWN
SURFACE
EMBELLISHMENT
PAGE 164

PAGE 165

PAGE 167
PAGE 168
PAGE 171

HAND-
SEWN
INSERTION
STITCHES
PAGE 179

PAGE 180
PAGE 181

PAGE 182
PAGE 183
PAGE 184
PAGE 185

STITCHES
FOR
MACHINE
QUILTING
PAGE 186

PAGE 187

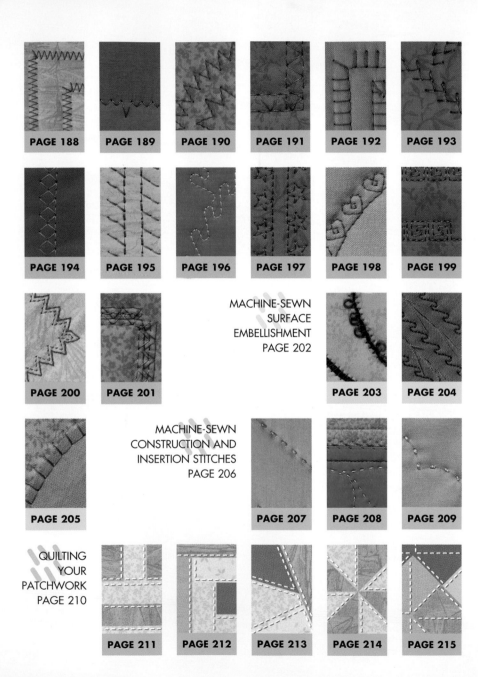

**PAGE 188**

**PAGE 189**

**PAGE 190**

**PAGE 191**

**PAGE 192**

**PAGE 193**

**PAGE 194**

**PAGE 195**

**PAGE 196**

**PAGE 197**

**PAGE 198**

**PAGE 199**

**PAGE 200**

**PAGE 201**

MACHINE-SEWN
SURFACE
EMBELLISHMENT
PAGE 202

**PAGE 203**

**PAGE 204**

MACHINE-SEWN
CONSTRUCTION AND
INSERTION STITCHES
PAGE 206

**PAGE 205**

**PAGE 207**

**PAGE 208**

**PAGE 209**

QUILTING
YOUR
PATCHWORK
PAGE 210

**PAGE 211**

**PAGE 212**

**PAGE 213**

**PAGE 214**

**PAGE 215**

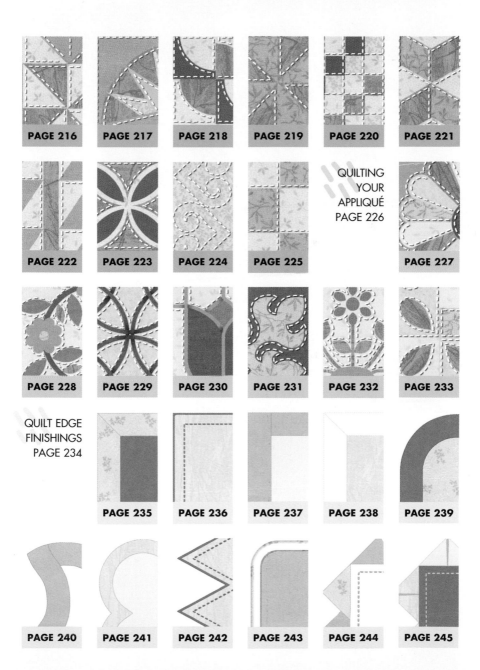

PAGE 216

PAGE 217

PAGE 218

PAGE 219

PAGE 220

PAGE 221

PAGE 222

PAGE 223

PAGE 224

PAGE 225

QUILTING
YOUR
APPLIQUÉ
PAGE 226

PAGE 227

PAGE 228

PAGE 229

PAGE 230

PAGE 231

PAGE 232

PAGE 233

QUILT EDGE
FINISHINGS
PAGE 234

PAGE 235

PAGE 236

PAGE 237

PAGE 238

PAGE 239

PAGE 240

PAGE 241

PAGE 242

PAGE 243

PAGE 244

PAGE 245

# Stitches for Hand Quilting

All quilters will be familiar with the traditional quilting stitch based on a running stitch. You can use the more interesting stitches shown here to add textural interest to your work.

All of these "alternative" quilting stitches can be sewn along a single quilting mark without the need to draw parallel tramlines. Any loops created by "threading" and "whipping" yarns can be left looser on decorative projects, or pulled tighter if used for a bed quilt.

If you sew with your left hand, many of the stitch diagrams will need to be worked in mirror image.

**REVERSE OF WORK**

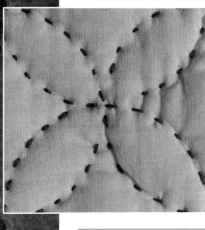

# *Running stitch*

Use this versatile stitch for hand quilting traditional designs and contour-quilting (outlining) motif patterns. Space stitches regularly, whether on straight or curved lines.

> ⑥ **TIPS**
>
> • Hold the needle almost perpendicular to the fabric to help you to take up all three layers.
> • Take several stitches on the needle at one time to help produce even stitching (more difficult to do on a tight curve).

**STEP 1**

*Begin by bringing the needle to the surface of the work.*

**STEP 2**

*Take two or three stitches forwards along the line, ensuring that the needle passes through all three layers of fabric with each stitch.*

**STEP 3**

*Pull the thread through until it lies on top of the fabric, without being too loose or too tight.*

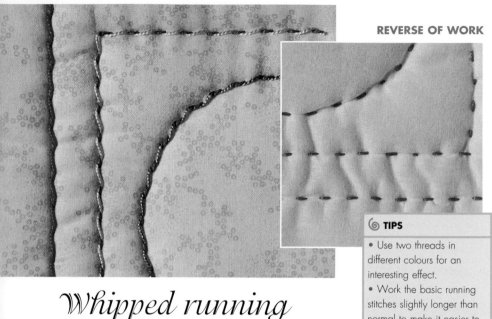

**REVERSE OF WORK**

## TIPS

- Use two threads in different colours for an interesting effect.
- Work the basic running stitches slightly longer than normal to make it easier to pass the whipping thread underneath them.
- Use the eye of the needle for whipping, or change to a blunt tapestry needle.

# Whipped running

This stitch has a slightly raised appearance and can be effective when a little definition is needed for quilting and/or outlining motif patterns.

## STEP 1

*Bring the needle to the surface of the work and sew a line of running stitch.*

## STEP 2

*Bring the whipping thread to the surface of the work, just below the centre of the first running stitch.*

## STEP 3

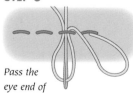

*Pass the eye end of the needle behind each individual running stitch in turn, working in the same direction each time.*

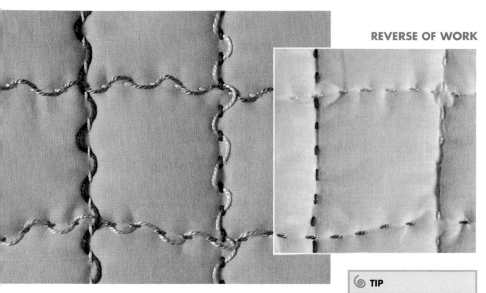

# Threaded running

A second thread snakes in and out of the running stitches, forming small loops: keep these tight if you are quilting a bed quilt, as they might snag and pull.

> **⑤ TIP**
>
> Use two threads in different colours for an interesting effect.

### STEP 1

*Bring the needle to the surface of the work and sew a line of running stitch.*

### STEP 2

*Bring the second thread to the surface of the work, close to the front of (or below the centre of) the first running stitch.*

### STEP 3

*Pass the eye end of the needle down behind the first running stitch and then up behind the second running stitch.*

### STEP 4

*Continue in this way along the row, alternating the direction of the needle with each stitch in turn.*

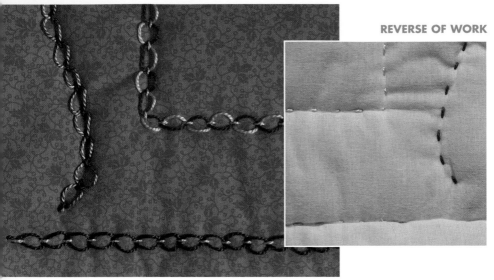

**REVERSE OF WORK**

# *Double threaded running*

This is very decorative in multiple colours. Support the previous stitches and loops with your other hand as you work. For a more dramatic effect, leave the loops slightly loose.

**STEP 1**

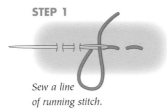

*Sew a line of running stitch.*

**STEP 2**

*Bring the second thread to the surface of the work at the beginning of the first stitch (or underneath at the centre point).*

**STEP 3**

*Pass the needle down behind the first stitch and up behind the second stitch; continue to the end of the row of stitches.*

**STEP 4**

*Bring the third thread up at the beginning of the work and weave behind each running stitch in the opposite direction.*

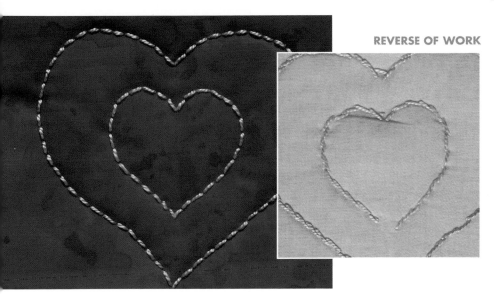

**REVERSE OF WORK**

# Backstitch

A good outlining and contouring stitch, which resembles a machined stitch. It is quite dense In appearance and so will give a solid feel and end result to your quilting.

**STEP 1**

*Bring the thread to the surface of the work, at the beginning of the quilting line.*

**STEP 2**

*Move a stitch length backwards along the line, take the needle down into the fabric and bring it back up to the surface approximately two stitch lengths further along the line.*

**STEP 3**

*Move back along the line and take the needle down into the same hole as the previous thread; bring it up approximately two stitch lengths further along the line. Continue to the end of the line.*

**REVERSE OF WORK**

# Stem stitch

Stem stitch is a popular outlining stitch and one
of the thicker stitches that can be successfully
used for quilting.

> **TIP**
>
> For a broader stitch, work it
> at a slight diagonal (take
> the needle in below the line
> and bring it to the surface
> above the line).

**STEP 1**

*Bring the thread to the
surface of the work, at
the beginning of the
quilting line.*

**STEP 3**

**STEP 2**

*Holding the thread below
the line with the thumb of
your non-sewing hand, take
a small stitch backwards
(i.e. facing towards the
starting point of the line).*

*Repeat the stitch along the line, ensuring that the
needle is brought up at the point at which the
thread of the previous stitch entered the fabric.
Don't forget to hold the thread below the line
with each stitch.*

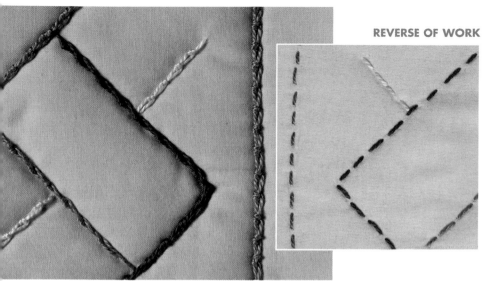

**REVERSE OF WORK**

# Portuguese knotted stem

This ideal outlining stitch has added textural interest. The knots are constructed from two whipping stitches on the surface of the work.

### STEP 1

Bring the needle to the surface of the work and, working upwards and away from you, take it in on the line and then back towards you, bringing it up at the halfway point and on the left of the stitch you have just made.

### STEP 2

With the thread above the needle, slide the needle (or eye of the needle) from right to left under the large stitch and pull the thread through to make the first wrap.

### STEP 3

With the thread above the needle again, slide the needle under the first stitch a second time, pulling the thread through and ensuring that the second wrap is beneath the first one. This forms a knot.

### STEP 4

To begin the second stitch, move along the line and take the stitch back towards yourself, bringing it up halfway and to the left of the large stitch, ready to start the two-stage wrapping sequence again.

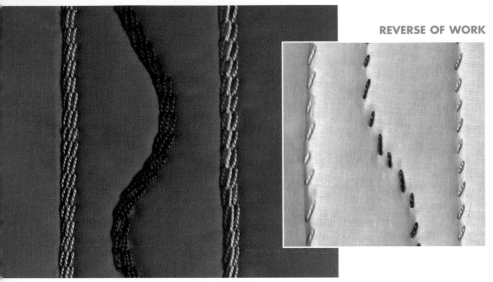

REVERSE OF WORK

# Raised stem

A ladder of base stitches is covered with stem stitch to give a raised appearance, entirely covered by working more rows.

## STEP 1

*Bring the thread to the surface of the work and stitch a row of base stitches to make a ladder – work from one side of the quilting line to the other, either horizontally or vertically (whichever you find easiest).*

## STEP 2

*Start the stem stitch: bring the wrapping thread to the surface of the work at the centre of the first ladder stitch. The stem stitch is worked on the surface of the work only.*

## STEP 3

*Hold the fabric so you are working "up" the ladder and take the needle down behind the first ladder. Pull the thread through and take the needle down behind the second ladder. Continue in this way.*

## STEP 4

*When you have reached the end of the row of base stitches, go back to the beginning and work another row of stem stitch. Continue working rows of stem stitch over the ladder of base stitches until you have achieved the desired result. Use the same colour of thread or change the colours for each row.*

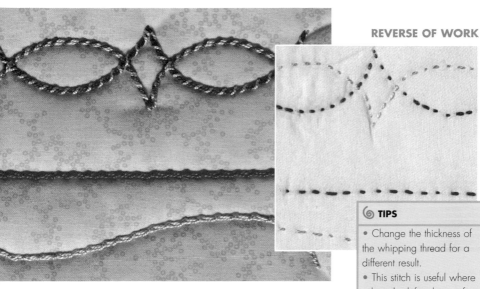

**REVERSE OF WORK**

## 🌀 TIPS

• Change the thickness of the whipping thread for a different result.
• This stitch is useful where a heavily defined row of quilting is required.
• Pass the eye of the needle through first, or use a blunt tapestry needle, to prevent catching fibres of fabric or thread.

# Whipped stem

A foundation row of stem stitch is whipped over with a second thread – this can be the same colour as the first thread or a different one for a more dramatic finished result.

### STEP 1

*Bring the thread to the surface of the work and sew a base line of stem stitch.*

### STEP 3

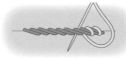

### STEP 2

*Thread the needle with the whipping thread and bring this to the surface of the work at one end of the base row of stem stitch.*

*Pass the needle down behind each stem stitch in turn, working in the same direction each time and avoiding catching up any fabric. Whip each stitch individually, pulling the thread through fully after each stitch.*

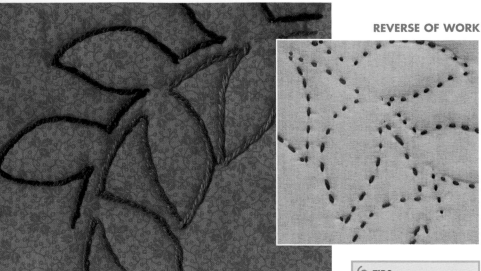

**REVERSE OF WORK**

# Outline stitch

Outline stitch is very versatile and useful for contour-quilting motifs as well as continuous line quilting designs, because it makes a neat twisted line.

**STEP 1**

*Bring the thread to the surface of the work, at the beginning of the quilting line. Holding the thread above the line, take a stitch back along the line towards your starting point.*

**STEP 2**

*Pull the thread through and make the next stitch: move further along the line, stitch back (ensuring that the needle comes up where the thread for the last stitch entered the fabric) and pull through.*

**STEP 3**

*Continue in this way along the line. The stitches will twist in the opposite direction to those of stem stitch.*

⚙ **TIPS**

• Use various thicknesses of thread for differing results.
• Always hold the thread above the needle – make use of the thumb on your non-sewing hand.
(This stitch is very similar to stem stitch, where the thread is always held below the needle.)

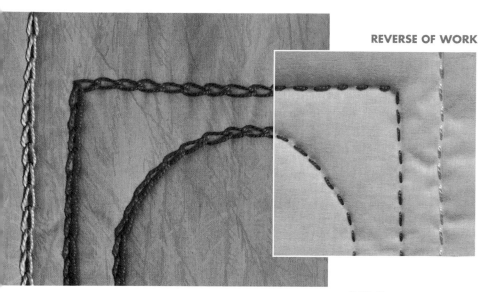

**REVERSE OF WORK**

# Chain stitch

This decorative stitch is equally effective worked in fine or thick thread. It is useful for continuous line designs as well as contour-quilting (outlining) motifs.

### STEP 1

Bring the thread to the surface of the work, at the beginning of the quilting line. Using the thumb of your non-sewing hand, hold the thread forwards along the line to form a loop. Take the needle back into the hole where the thread was initially brought out; at the same time, take a stitch forwards along the line.

### STEP 2

Bring the needle up inside the waiting loop of thread, pull the thread through and hold the thread along the line to form a loop ready for the next stitch.

### STEP 3

Take the needle down into the hole (or very slightly to one side of it) where the thread last came out – this will be inside the previous chain sewn.

### STEP 4

Take a stitch forwards and bring the needle up into the waiting loop of thread.

Continue in this way, securing the final chain with a small stitch outside the last chain that you sew.

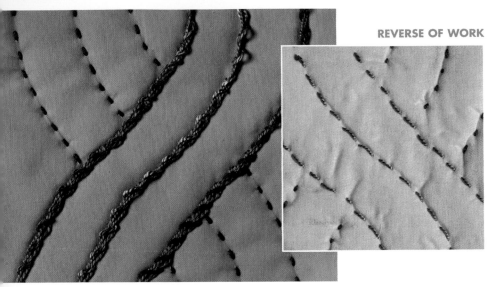

**REVERSE OF WORK**

# Whipped chain stitch

Whipping a row of chain stitch will change the original stitches quite dramatically. The end result will resemble a decorative plait sitting on the surface of the work.

**STEP 1**

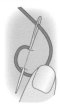

*Bring the thread to the surface of the work, at the beginning of the quilting line, and sew a base line of chain stitch (see page 77).*

**STEP 3**

*Pass the needle under each full chain stitch in turn, working in the same direction each time and being careful not to pull the whipping thread too tight.*

**STEP 2**

*Bring the whipping thread to the surface of the work at the beginning of the first chain stitch.*

**STEP 4**

*Carry on in this way along the row of chain stitch. Use a finer thread if you want the chain stitch to show through more, and a thicker thread if you want the resulting "plait" to look heavier.*

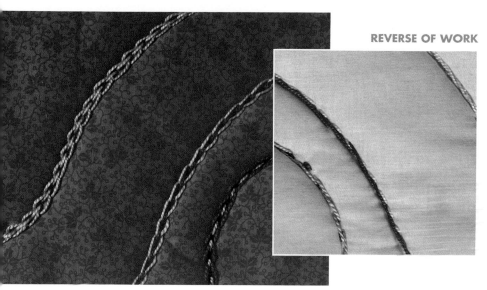

**REVERSE OF WORK**

# Backstitched chain

The chain links are oversewn with backstitch worked in the same colour and thickness of thread, or a contrasting colour and/or thickness for a more decorative effect.

## STEP 1

Work a foundation row of chain stitch (see page 77). Bring the thread to the surface of the work, at the beginning of the quilting line. Hold the thread forwards and take a quilting stitch through all layers, forwards along the line, bringing the needle up into the waiting loop of thread. Repeat along the line, taking the needle into each previous chain in turn, with each stitch.

## STEP 2

Now work the backstitch (see page 71) row. Bring the second/contrast thread to the surface of the work at the beginning of the chain stitch row. Take the needle into the first link of the chain and stitch forwards, bringing the needle up in the second link.

## STEP 3

Take the needle down in the first link again, and stitch forwards two links to come up inside the third link. Progress along the line in this way, securing the second/contrast thread outside one of the chain stitch links.

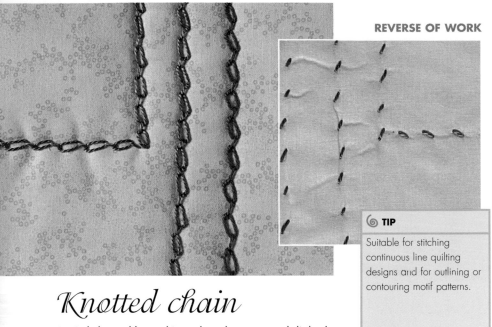

**REVERSE OF WORK**

**TIP**

Suitable for stitching continuous line quilting designs and for outlining or contouring motif patterns.

# Knotted chain

A stitch formed by making a knot between each link of a line of chain stitch, produced by twisting the thread in a certain way. This stitch has a slightly zigzag finished appearance.

**STEP 1**

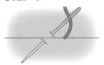

Bring the thread out at the beginning of the quilting line. Take a diagonal stitch forwards, in above the line and out below.

**STEP 2**

Hold the thread forwards and pass the needle behind the diagonal stitch, without taking up any fabric. Pull the thread through and adjust the loop as necessary.

**STEP 3**

Hold the thread forwards and pass the needle through the loop of thread without taking up any fabric.

**STEP 4**

Support the loop with your free thumb while taking the next diagonal stitch. Repeat steps 1, 2 and 3 to continue along the quilting line.

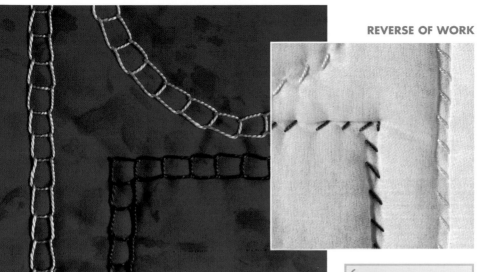

**REVERSE OF WORK**

# Open chain

This variation on chain stitch gives an open, ladder-like result. Work the stitches down towards you to help to get the stitches even.

> **⑥ TIP**
>
> Always use the thumb on your non-sewing hand to hold the thread so the complete stitch does not collapse sideways.

**STEP 1**

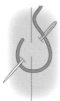

*Bring the thread out to the left of the quilting line. Hold it forwards so it forms a loop. Take the needle in on the right of the line (level with the left-hand thread) and take a diagonal stitch forwards, bringing the needle out on the left of the line and into the waiting loop of thread.*

**STEP 2**

*Hold the thread forwards to form the next loop. Use the needle to stretch the previous chain sideways, take the needle inside the last (stretched) chain and take a diagonal stitch forwards again, bringing the needle up on the left of the line and into the waiting loop of thread.*

**STEP 3**

*Continue in this way. Secure the very last open chain with two tiny securing stitches, so you finish with a square stitch or "box".*

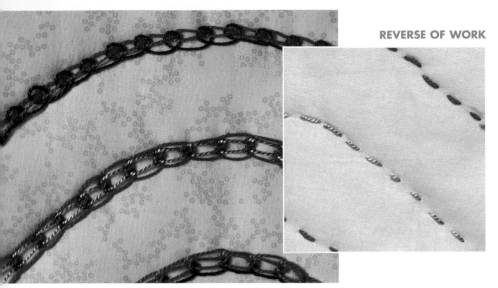

**REVERSE OF WORK**

# Interlaced chain

Work one row of interlacing to one side of the chain, or a row on both sides to give a more symmetrical result. The interlacing does not go through the fabric.

## STEP 1

*Bring the thread out at the beginning of the quilting line and stitch a foundation row of plain chain stitch (see page 77).*

## STEP 2

*Bring the second (lacing) thread to the surface of the work at the beginning of the first chain stitch.*

## STEP 3

*Take the needle up and under the bottom part of the second chain stitch in line, then come down behind the bottom part (and the lacing thread) of the first chain stitch.*

## STEP 4

*Take the needle up and under the bottom part of the third chain stitch, then come down behind the bottom part (and the lacing thread) of the second chain stitch. Continue in this manner – two chains forwards and one back.*

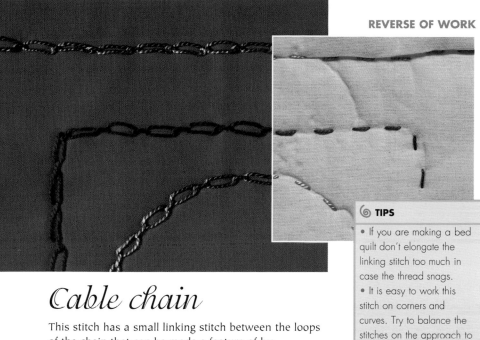

**REVERSE OF WORK**

**⑥ TIPS**

• If you are making a bed quilt don't elongate the linking stitch too much in case the thread snags.
• It is easy to work this stitch on corners and curves. Try to balance the stitches on the approach to a corner so the chains are even.

# Cable chain

This stitch has a small linking stitch between the loops of the chain that can be made a feature of by elongating it or shortening the link.

**STEP 1**

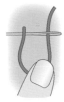

*Work this stitch down towards you. Bring the thread out at the start of the quilting line. Hold it forwards along the line and pass the needle behind it.*

**STEP 2**

*Hold the thread on the surface of the fabric with your non-sewing thumb, and with a twist, bring the needle forwards over the thread again and into the fabric, take a quilting stitch (through all layers) forwards along the line, and bring the needle back up into the waiting loop of thread.*

**STEP 3**

*Continue in this way along the quilting line. Finish with a small securing stitch outside the last chain.*

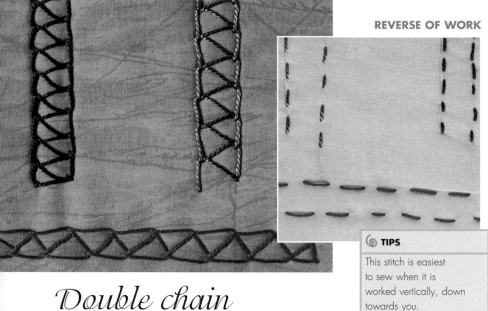

## 🌀 TIPS

This stitch is easiest to sew when it is worked vertically, down towards you.

# Double chain

This wide stitch should be used in areas of a design where there is plenty of space. Don't be tempted to work it too wide, as it would then distort the fabric.

## STEP 1

Bring the thread to the surface of the work, on the left of the quilting line. Hold the thread forwards (in the direction in which the needle will travel) and over to the right, and take a vertical quilting stitch (through all layers) towards you and on the right of the line, bringing the needle into the waiting loop of thread.

## STEP 2

Hold the thread forwards and over to the left, take a vertical quilting stitch, taking the needle in at the same point that the thread started, and stitching forwards and towards you, passing the level of the right-hand thread point.

## STEP 3

Hold the thread forwards and over to the right, take the needle into the fabric behind the last stitch sewn and stitch forwards and towards you into the waiting loop of thread. Continue in this way, finishing with a small securing stitch to hold the final triangle open.

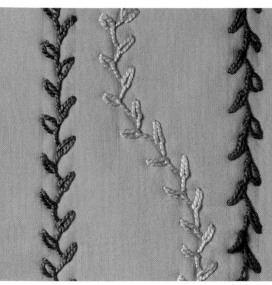

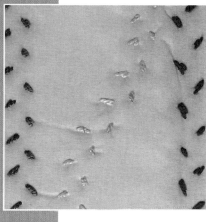

# *Feathered chain*

This decorative stitch consists of little diagonal chains that resemble leaves on a trellis. The feathering can be worked narrow or wide.

## STEP 1

*Bring the thread to the surface of the work and on the right-hand side of the quilting line. Hold the thread forwards and round to the right, insert the needle in the same place it came out and take a small chain stitch forwards, bringing the needle up into the waiting loop of thread to form a chain.*

## STEP 2

*Take the needle in on the left of the quilting line and stitch diagonally backwards and up to the left.*

## STEP 3

*Insert the needle into the same place it came out and, holding the thread forwards and round to the right, take a small chain stitch forwards, bringing the needle up at the same place the previous thread went in, and into the waiting loop of thread to form a chain.*

## STEP 4

*Take a backwards, diagonal stitch to the right and repeat stages 1, 2 and 3. Continue working along the line and finish with a small securing stitch outside the last chain stitch.*

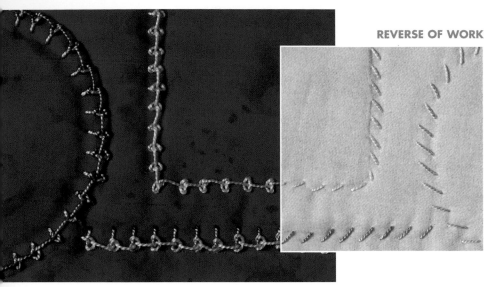

**REVERSE OF WORK**

# Raised chain

There are two stages to this stitch: making a ladder, then wrapping or knotting it – these stitches can be worked in the same thread or contrasting colours.

**STEP 1**

Bring the thread to the surface of the fabric and stitch a row of horizontal quilting stitches (passing through all layers).

**STEP 2**

Bring the second (wrapping) thread to the surface, on the quilting line and central to the ladder of horizontal stitches. Pass the needle up and under the first stitch on the ladder (do not catch the fabric).

**STEP 3**

Holding the thread down and around to the right to form a loop, take the needle down behind the first stitch on the ladder and into the waiting loop of thread.

**STEP 4**

Repeat stages 2 and 3 as you progress along the ladder.

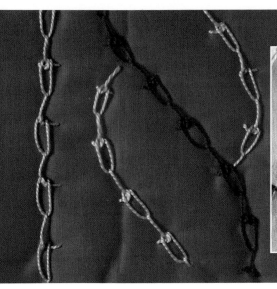

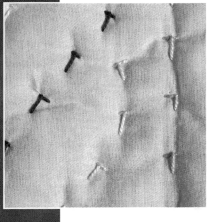

# *Knotted cable*

This stitch is based on coral stitch and chain stitch, with an intriguing and ornate raised knot between each link in the chain. It has a slightly zigzag finished appearance.

### STEP 1

*Bring the thread to the surface of the work, at the beginning of the quilting line. You will be working horizontally and from right to left. Hold the thread forwards along the line and looped down and backwards. Take a small vertical quilting stitch downwards through all layers, bringing the needle out below the line. Pull the thread through.*

### STEP 2

*Pass the needle under the existing stitch without catching up any of the fabric.*

### STEP 3

*Hold the thread forwards and downwards and take a small horizontal stitch forwards above the line.*

### STEP 4

*Repeat steps 1, 2 and 3 to progress along the quilting line. Finish the thread outside a knot or a chain stitch to secure the work.*

**REVERSE OF WORK**

# Twisted chain

This is a more textured variation of basic chain stitch. It is quite narrow, so useful for continuous line designs and outlining or contour-quilting around motifs.

**STEP 1**

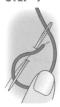

*Bring the thread to the surface of the fabric, at the beginning of the quilting line. Hold the thread forwards along the line, and take the needle in above the thread and to the left of the line. Bring the needle out below the thread, to the right of the line and into the waiting loop. The chain will twist automatically.*

**STEP 2**

*Hold the thread forwards along the line and repeat for the next stitch. Continue along the line and finish with a small securing stitch outside the final chain.*

## ⓖ TIPS

• Don't be tempted to make the loops of the chain too long, or they will become quite narrow and lose the effect of a linked chain.

• As with all chain stitch variations, make use of the thumb on your non-sewing hand to place the thread to form a loop, ready for the next stitch.

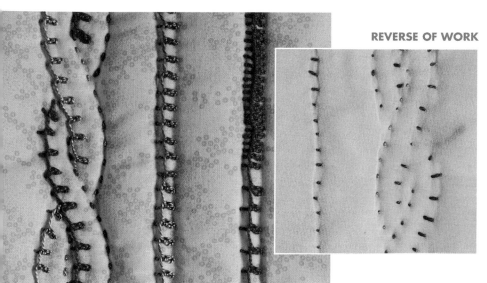

**REVERSE OF WORK**

# *Rosette chain*

This wide stitch produces a decorative result similar to a plait. Don't make the stitch too wide – it will become too unstable for use in quilting.

### STEP 1

*Working horizontally, bring the thread to the surface of the work, above the quilting line. Take a vertical stitch (in above the line and out below the line) and hold the thread so it wraps forwards and around and under the needle. Pull the thread through and hold the stitch with the thumb of your non-sewing hand while you continue.*

### STEP 2

*Take the needle upwards, underneath the starting thread, without catching the fabric.*

### STEP 3

*Make the next vertical stitch, in above the line and out below the line, wrapping the thread forwards and around and under the needle.*

### STEP 4

*Continue as before, this time passing the needle upwards under the existing bar of thread that is sitting between the two looped chains. Finish with a small securing stitch outside the final chain loop.*

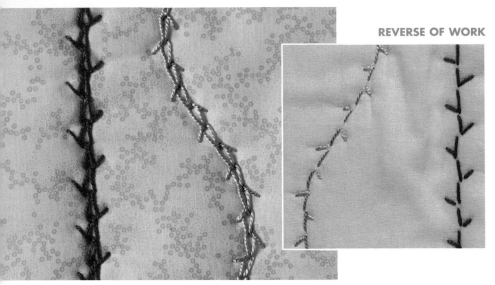

**REVERSE OF WORK**

# *Spine chain*

Once you have practised chain stitch (see page 77), it is easy to make the extra, intermittent diagonal stitches to add more movement to your work.

**STEP 3**

**STEP 1**

*Bring the thread to the surface of the work, at the beginning of the quilting line. Holding the thread forwards and looped around, take the needle into the same place as the thread emerged. Make a quilting stitch forwards along the line through all layers, bringing the needle up on the line and into the waiting loop of thread.*

**STEP 2**

*Now take the needle into the fabric on the right-hand side of the line, slightly further back. Stitch diagonally down and inwards, towards the line, bringing the needle up inside the first chain that you have sewn (do not loop the thread at this stage).*

*Holding the thread forwards along the line and looped around, take the needle inside the previous chain and stitch forwards along the line, bringing the needle up inside the waiting loop of thread. Now make a diagonal stitch on the left-hand side, bringing the needle up inside the previous chain. Continue in this way along the quilting line, finishing with a chain stitch or a diagonal stitch. Secure the thread outside the last chain.*

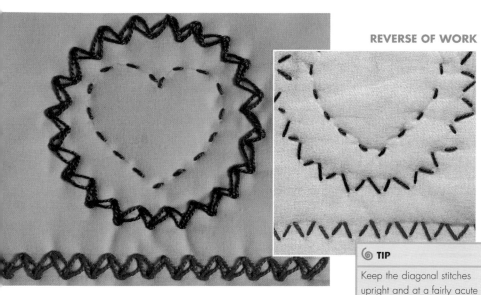

**REVERSE OF WORK**

**⑥ TIP**

Keep the diagonal stitches upright and at a fairly acute diagonal to the quilting line.

# Zigzag chain

This stitch can be found on very old embroideries. When worked very small, it will resemble a decorative plait laid on the fabric, rather than an obvious chain stitch.

## STEP 1

*Bring the thread to the surface of the work, just below the quilting line. Working horizontally, hold the thread forwards and around in front of the needle, to form a loop. Insert the needle at the same spot (or slightly to one side of) the thread originally came out of and make a quilting stitch diagonally upwards (through all layers), bringing the needle out above the quilting line and up into the waiting loop of thread.*

## STEP 2

*Hold the thread forwards to form a loop again. This time, pierce the thread of the previous chain and stitch diagonally downwards, bringing the needle out below the line and into the waiting loop of thread.*

## STEP 3

*Continue working either side of the line, alternating one stitch upwards with one stitch downwards. Secure the last chain with a small stitch outside the chain loop.*

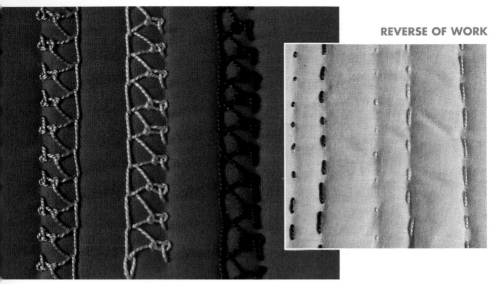

# Crested chain

This combination of chain and coral stitches can be worked horizontally (as shown below) or vertically. Leave space between stitches to achieve a lacy effect.

**STEP 1**

Bring the thread to the surface of the work. Form a loop and take the needle into the same place that the thread came out of the fabric. Make a horizontal quilting stitch forwards bringing the needle out into the waiting loop of thread.

**STEP 2**

Hold the thread above the work and loop it forwards and down. Make a quilting stitch forwards into the waiting loop of thread.

**STEP 3**

Pass the thread forwards and behind the central bar of thread that is sitting between the top and bottom stitches (do not catch any fabric).

**STEP 4**

Hold the thread forwards and looped down and around. Take the needle into the previous chain sewn and make a quilting stitch forwards, into the waiting loop of thread. Repeat stages 2, 3 and 4 and continue along the quilting line. Finish with a small securing stitch outside the last chain.

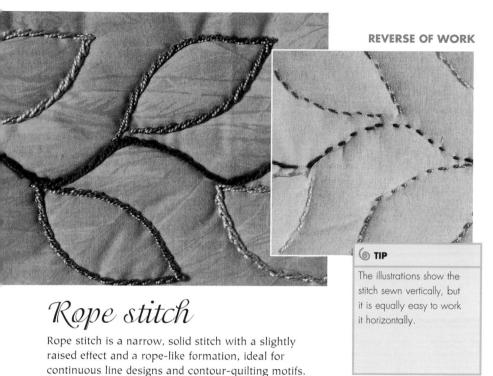

**REVERSE OF WORK**

# Rope stitch

Rope stitch is a narrow, solid stitch with a slightly raised effect and a rope-like formation, ideal for continuous line designs and contour-quilting motifs.

> ### ⑥ TIP
> The illustrations show the stitch sewn vertically, but it is equally easy to work it horizontally.

### STEP 1

*Bring the thread to the surface of the work, on the quilting line. Hold it forwards and around so it loops to the right. Take the needle in to the left of the thread emerging from the fabric and make a quilting stitch forwards (through all layers), bringing the needle up again further along the line and into the waiting loop of thread.*

### STEP 2

*Hold the thread forwards and around to the right. This time, take the needle slightly to the left of the line and also halfway back along the previous stitch. Tuck it in snugly alongside the previous stitch. Take a very slight diagonal stitch this time, bringing the needle out on the line again and into the waiting loop of thread.*

### STEP 3

*Carry on along the quilting line and secure the last knot or loop with a small securing stitch.*

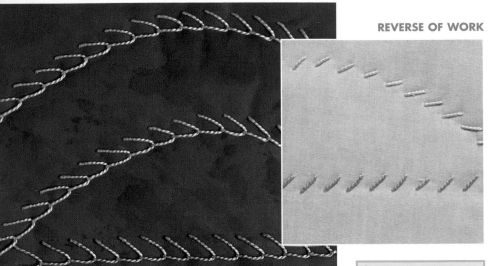

**REVERSE OF WORK**

# Half feather

Incredibly easy to sew, half feather stitch can add a lot of movement to a quilting design while being sewn speedily and fluidly.

### STEP 1

*Bring the thread to the surface of the work, at the beginning of the quilting line. Hold the thread down on the line and, working towards you, take the needle into the fabric on the right of the line. Make a quilting stitch diagonally forwards and bring the needle up on the line, into the waiting loop of thread.*

### STEP 2

*Again, hold the thread down on the line with the thumb of your non-sewing hand and make the next quilting stitch, sewing diagonally forwards and bringing the needle up on the line inside the waiting loop of thread.*

> 🌀 **TIP**
>
> Keep the needle at quite an acute angle, to emphasize the angle of the stitches and ensure that they stay at a diagonal.

### STEP 3

*Continue in this way until you have reached the end of the design or thread. Finish the work with a small securing stitch outside the last stitch to be sewn.*

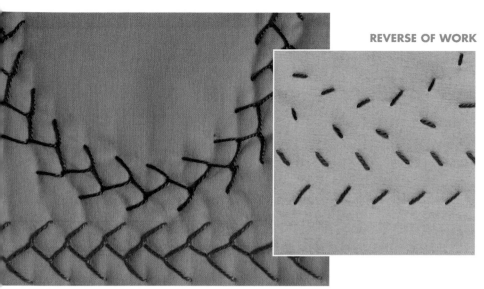

**REVERSE OF WORK**

# Single feather

The delicate and attractive appearance of this stitch can be further enhanced by varying the angle of the needle and the length and spacing of the stitches.

### STEP 1

Bring the thread to the surface of the work, at the beginning of the quilting line. Working down towards you, hold the thread down on the line and looped around to the right. Make a quilting stitch (through all layers) on the right of the line, stitching diagonally downwards and inwards towards the line, but not actually touching it, and bringing the needle up into the waiting loop of thread.

### STEP 2

Hold the thread down on the line and now loop it around to the left. Make a quilting stitch on the left of the line, taking the needle into the fabric level with where the thread last came out on the right. Stitch diagonally down and inwards towards the line, without actually touching it, and bring the needle up into the waiting loop of thread.

### STEP 3

Carry on in this way, working either side of the line, but not actually touching it. This will help you to achieve the little pattern that resembles bird's footprints. Finish with a small securing stitch outside the last V-shaped stitch.

**REVERSE OF WORK**

# Double feather

This is a wider variation of single feather stitch. The result is a decorative, feathery line that is more ornate than the narrower, "bird tracks" appearance of single feather stitch.

## STEP 1

*Bring the thread to the surface of the work and to the left of the quilting line. Hold the thread down towards you and looped around to the right. Make a quilting stitch (through all layers), stitching diagonally downwards and inwards from right to left, and bringing the needle up into the waiting loop of thread. Repeat to make a second stitch, working diagonally inwards from right to left.*

## STEP 2

*Hold the thread down towards you and now loop it around to the left. Make a quilting stitch to the left of the previous stitches, taking the needle into the fabric level – where the thread last came out on the right. Stitch diagonally down and inwards, bringing the needle up into the waiting loop of thread. Hold the thread down and around to the left and make another stitch, working diagonally inwards from left to right.*

## STEP 3

*Carry on in this way, working two feather stitches on the right and two on the left.*

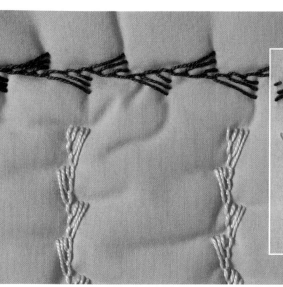

**REVERSE OF WORK**

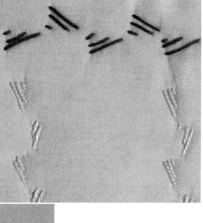

# *Maidenhair*

A decorative variation of basic single feather stitch, which is concentrated on a single central line. Keep the longest, outer branches tucked well in against their neighbours.

**STEP 1**

*Bring the thread to the surface of the work, at the beginning of the quilting line. Working vertically, down towards you, hold the thread down on the line and around to the right with your non-sewing thumb.*

*Make a diagonal quilting stitch through all layers, working in from the right of the line, stitching down and inwards towards the line, bringing the needle up on the line and into the waiting loop of thread.*

**STEP 2**

*Hold the thread in the same way and do a second diagonal stitch. Keep the top of the stitch level with the branch of the first one and bring the needle out on the line into the waiting loop of thread.*

**STEP 3**

*Make a third stitch in the same way, tucking the needle in close to the previous stitches on the line.*

**STEP 4**

*Now hold the thread down and to the left. Repeat the sequence of stitches, working in from the left. Continue working three stitches either side of the line.*

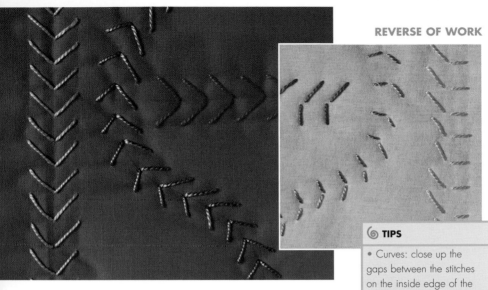

**REVERSE OF WORK**

# Arrowhead

A versatile and speedy quilting stitch, which is simple to sew on a straight line and even easier to sew on a gently curving line. It bears a slight resemblance to fly stitch (see page 99).

(see page 99)

**⑥ TIPS**

• Curves: close up the gaps between the stitches on the inside edge of the curve; space them slightly further apart on the outside edge of the curve.
• Spacing: ideally, have the top points of each V-shape level with the bottom point of the previous V-shape. If a more densely stitched effect is required, sew closer together.

**STEP 1**

*Bring the thread to the surface of the work, on the left of the quilting line. Take the needle in on the line, a little further down than your starting point, and make a diagonal stitch upwards and out to the right of the line.*

**STEP 2**

*Pull the thread through. Take the needle into where the thread previously went in and stitch horizontally, out to the left of the line.*

**STEP 3**

*Pull the thread through and repeat the first two stages, progressing along the line. Finish with a complete V-shaped stitch.*

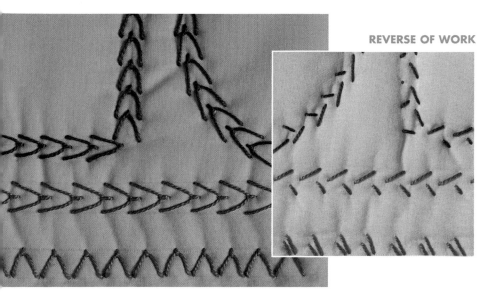

**REVERSE OF WORK**

# *Fly stitch*

This stitch can be sewn horizontally or vertically; it can also be used as a filling stitch. It can form a "Y" (longer securing stitch) or a "V" shape (shorter securing stitch).

**STEP 1**

Bring the thread to the surface of the work, on the left of the quilting line. Hold the thread downwards and looped around to the right. Take the needle in on the right-hand side of the line (level with where the thread started on the left) and make a quilting stitch through all layers, at a downwards diagonal, bringing the needle up on the line and into the waiting loop of thread.

**STEP 2**

Take the needle back into the layers, on the line and underneath the V-shaped stitch that you have just sewn. Bring the needle up on the left-hand side of the line.

**STEP 3**

Repeat these two stages. Ensure that the thread is held down and looped around. Carry on along the quilting line and secure the last V-shaped stitch when you finish off.

**STEP 4**

When working along a horizontal line, work above and below the quilting line.

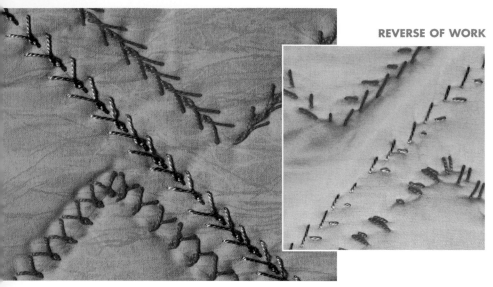

**REVERSE OF WORK**

# Twisted fly

This has a decorative twist in the thread below each fly stitch, which provides added textural interest. For a denser effect, work the stitches closer together.

**STEP 1**

Bring the thread to the surface of the work, on the left of the quilting line. Hold it downwards and looped around to the right. Take the needle in on the right-hand side of the line (level with where the thread started on the left) and make a quilting stitch through all layers, at a downwards diagonal, bringing the needle up on the line and underneath the waiting thread loop.

**STEP 2**

Keep the loop of thread in place and pass the needle over the top of it and behind it.

**STEP 3**

Take the needle into the fabric on the quilting line and make a quilting stitch out to the left of the line to start again. Carry on along the line and finish with a central securing stitch.

**ALTERNATIVE**

This stitch can also be worked horizontally. Instead of working either side of the line, work

above and below it in the same manner as horizontal fly stitch (see page 99).

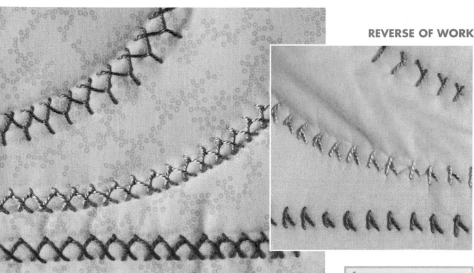

**REVERSE OF WORK**

# *Plaited fly*

Plaited fly stitch needs to be sewn horizontally along the quilting line so the branches of the individual stitches overlap. It is very easy to keep this stitch even.

> (◎ **TIP**
>
> It is possible to elongate or shorten the securing stitch in the centre of each V shape; however, there is not a lot of scope for altering the spacing between the stitches.

### STEP 1

*Work horizontally, from left to right. Bring the thread to the surface of the work, above the quilting line. Hold it downwards and around to the right. Take the needle in above the quilting line, slightly further along the work and level with the starting point. Make a quilting stitch at a diagonal, downwards and inwards, bringing the needle up on the line and into the waiting loop of thread.*

### STEP 2

*Take the needle into the fabric under the line and centrally under the V shape. Make a vertical quilting stitch upwards, bringing the needle out above the line level with the two branches of the "V".*

### STEP 3

*Make a second fly stitch and progress along the work, overlapping the branches of the fly stitches as you go. Secure the work with the thread outside and below the last V-shaped fly stitch.*

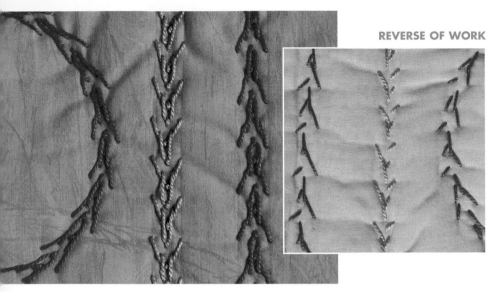

**REVERSE OF WORK**

# Double fly

The basic fly stitch has to be stitched at quite an exaggerated length to enable a second, narrower fly stitch to sit inside and overlap the first.

**STEP 1**

Bring the thread to the surface of the work and to the left-hand side of the quilting line. Working horizontally and down towards you, hold the thread so it loops down and around to the right. Take the needle in on the right of the line and make a quilting stitch through all layers, diagonally downwards and inwards towards the line, bringing the needle up on the line and into the waiting loop of thread.

**STEP 2**

Take the needle in on the line, beneath the V-shaped stitch that you have produced, and bring it out inside the previous fly stitch.

**STEP 3**

Hold thread down and to the right. Take the needle in on the right and stitch diagonally, bringing the needle up on the line, below the previous stitch and into a loop of thread.

**STEP 4**

Repeat these combined stitches, working along the quilting line. Finish with a complete double fly stitch and secure the thread outside the last V-shaped stitch.

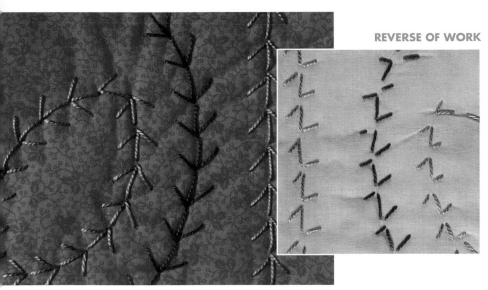

**REVERSE OF WORK**

# Fern stitch

This pretty line can be worked with all three points of the "fern" level with each other, or with the central point of the "fern" higher and the two outside stitches lower.

**STEP 1**

*Bring the thread to the surface of the work, on the quilting line. Take the needle out further up and to the right of the line. Make a quilting stitch through all layers, diagonally upwards (or horizontally for a level "fern" – see step 4 picture) and pull the thread through.*

**STEP 2**

*Take the needle in at the starting point again and stitch diagonally upwards and out to the left.*

**STEP 3**

*Take the needle in at the starting point once more and stitch down towards you, coming out on the line again, ready to start the next complete stitch.*

**STEP 4**

*To make the tops of the stitches level, make a horizontal stitch at step 1, and a sharper diagonal stitch at step 2.*

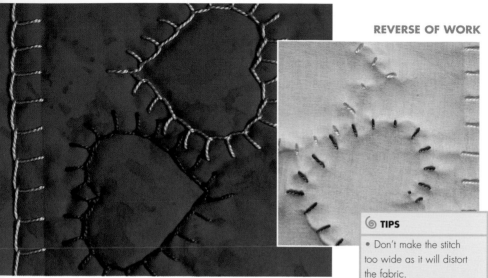

**REVERSE OF WORK**

## 🌀 TIPS

• Don't make the stitch too wide as it will distort the fabric.

• If the stitches are too close together, they will resemble buttonhole stitch, which may be too dense.

• Curves and circles: different effects can be achieved, depending on whether the "spikes" are on the outside or inside of the curve.

# *Blanket stitch*

This fast, simple stitch is often used for edging fabric and for overstitching raw edges of appliqué. It can add quite a lot of movement to a project.

### STEP 1

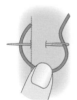

Bring the thread to the surface of the work at the start of the quilting line and on the line itself. Hold the thread down on the line and, working towards you, make a quilting stitch through all layers from right to left, bringing the needle back up on the line and into the waiting loop of thread.

### STEP 2

Hold the thread down on the line and stitch from right to left again.

### STEP 3

Work along the line in this way, spacing the stitches evenly. Finish the row of stitches with a small securing stitch outside the last blanket stitch, to hold the shape.

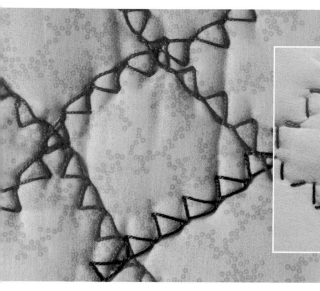

**REVERSE OF WORK**

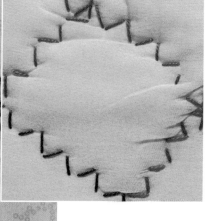

# Closed blanket

It is easiest to work this stitch vertically down towards you, because of the angles required to form it. Vary the spaces within the triangles by making the diagonal stitches deeper or shallower.

**STEP 1**

*Bring the thread to the surface of the work at the start of the quilting line and on the line itself. Hold the thread down on the line and take the needle in to the right of the line, making a quilting stitch through all layers upwards and diagonally in towards the line, bringing the needle out on the line again and into the waiting loop of thread. Pull the thread through.*

**STEP 2**

*Hold the thread down on the line and take the needle in at the same place. Make a diagonal stitch downwards and in towards the line, bringing the needle out on the line and into the waiting loop of thread. Pull the thread through.*

**STEP 3**

*Hold the thread down on the line, take the needle in on the right of the line and stitch diagonally upwards and in towards the line, bringing the needle into the waiting loop of thread but outside the previously formed triangle. Pull the thread through. Repeat step 2 to complete this second stitch. Continue working along the line and finish with a securing stitch outside the last triangle.*

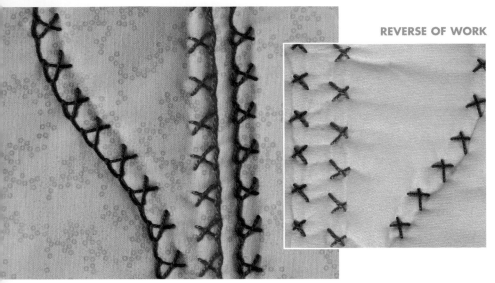

**REVERSE OF WORK**

# Crossed blanket

The two branches of each stitch overlap to create a cross on the surface of the work, separated by a bar stitch that can be elongated or reduced as desired.

## STEP 1

Bring the thread to the surface of the work, at the beginning of the quilting line. Working vertically and down towards you, hold the thread down on the line and looped around to the right. Make a quilting stitch through all layers, taking the needle in to the right of the line and stitching diagonally upwards/backwards along the line, bringing the needle out on the line and into the waiting loop of thread.

## STEP 2

Holding the thread down on the line and looped around to the right again, take the needle back in on the right and about a stitch length above/away from the previous stitch. Make a diagonal quilting stitch downwards/forwards, bringing the needle up on the line and into the waiting loop of thread.

## STEP 3

Repeat steps 1 and 2 to progress along the quilting line, spacing the individual stitches evenly. Finish the thread outside the "second" part of a stitch to secure the work.

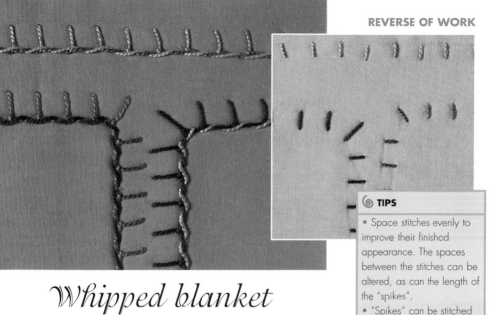

**REVERSE OF WORK**

# Whipped blanket

Whipping a row of blanket stitch adds a slightly raised effect to the lower edge of the stitch; you can make a feature of this by using a contrasting thread.

**STEP 1**

*Bring the thread to the surface of the work, at the start of the quilting line and on the line itself. Work a row of blanket stitch (see page 104).*

**STEP 2**

*Bring the second or contrasting thread to the surface of the work at the beginning of the row of blanket stitch and at the same starting point. Pass the needle under each straight bar stitch in turn, in the same direction each time.*

**STEP 3**

*For corners, carry on in the same way – the whipping thread and stitches will fall into place.*

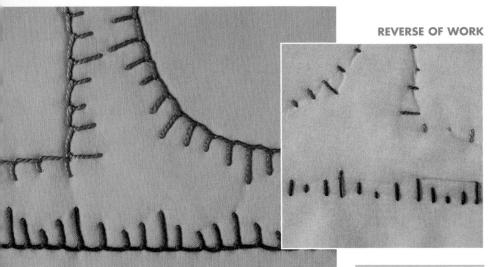

**REVERSE OF WORK**

# Long and short blanket

You can have a lot of fun with plain blanket stitch (see page 104) simply by altering the length and width of the stitches, or clustering the stitches together more closely.

**STEP 1**

Bring the thread to the surface of the work, at the start of the quilting line and on the line itself. Hold the thread down on the line and take the needle into the fabric on the right of the quilting line. Make a stitch in towards the line and bring the needle up on the line into the waiting loop of thread. Pull the thread through.

**⑤ TIP**

Don't make the longer stitches too wide because this will distort the fabric.

**STEP 2**

Repeat the stitch as above, but make the next stitch slightly wider, or shorter, according to how you would like your work to look.

**STEP 3**

Carry on along the quilting line and finish with a small securing stitch outside the last blanket stitch to be sewn.

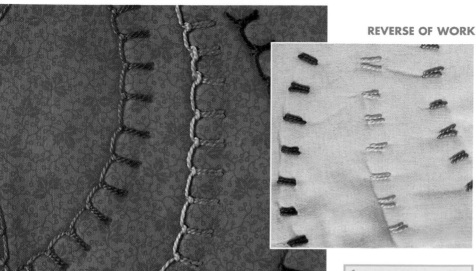

# *Up and down blanket*

This has a heavier finished appearance than basic blanket stitch (see page 104). Two stitches sit close to each other and give a more raised effect at the stitch base.

### STEP 1

*Bring the thread to the surface of the work, at the start of your quilting line and on the line itself. Hold the thread so it is looped down and around to the right. Take the needle into the fabric above the line, make a quilting stitch downwards and bring the needle up on the line and into the waiting loop of thread. Pull the thread through.*

### STEP 2

*Hold the thread upwards and to the right. Take the needle in on the line, directly next to the point at which the thread last came out of the fabric. Make a quilting stitch upwards, bringing the needle out level with the last stitch, directly alongside it and into the waiting loop of thread.*

### ⑥ TIPS

• Ensure that the two stitches sit as close together as possible without using the same fabric entry point.
• It may take a little while to get used to turning the needle from one direction to the other, but a little practice will make perfect.

### STEP 3

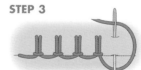

*Repeat these two stages to work along the line. Finish with an upwards stitch and a small securing stitch outside the last stitch.*

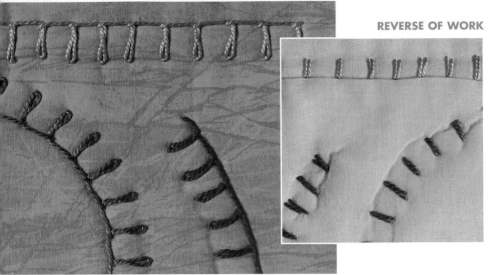

**REVERSE OF WORK**

# Basque stitch

One of the more unusual stitches used for quilting, originating in Spain, where it was traditionally worked with red thread on green fabric, or white thread on blue-green fabric.

## STEP 1

Bring the thread to the surface of the work, at the beginning of the quilting line. Working horizontally and from left to right, make a deep, vertical quilting stitch through all layers. Take the needle in on the line and bring it out below the line but, before the needle is pulled through, wrap the thread behind the eye of the needle from left to right, across the front of the needle from right to left and around behind the pointed end of the needle from left to right. Hold this firmly while the needle and thread are both pulled through.

## STEP 2

Keep your non-sewing thumb on this loop of thread while you make a second quilting stitch, vertically upwards, taking the needle in below the stitched loop to secure it and back up to the quilting line, bringing the needle in to the left of the loop and below the bar of thread at the top.

## STEP 3

Repeat steps 1 and 2 to progress along the quilting line, finishing the thread after an upwards vertical stitch and outside the last loop.

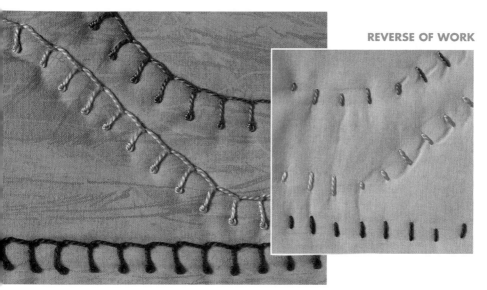

**REVERSE OF WORK**

# Knotted blanket

An extra twist is added to the thread to form a small, decorative and tactile knot, which sits on the surface of the work at the top of the "spikes" of the blanket stitch.

**STEP 1**

*Bring the thread to the surface of the work, at the beginning of and above the quilting line. Wrap the thread around your non-sewing thumb (the one that is not holding the needle): bring the thread around the right-hand side of the thumb, across the front to the left, around the back to the right and let it cross over itself. At this stage, take the needle upwards and behind the thread passing over the front of your thumb.*

**STEP 2**

*In one movement, gently slip the twisted thread off your thumb and take the needle into the fabric above the line. Make a quilting stitch down towards the line, and bring the needle up on the line and into the waiting loop of thread. The twisted thread will form a knot at the top of the "spike".*

**STEP 3**

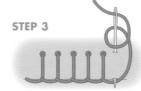

*Repeat this along the quilting line; finish with a small securing stitch outside the last stitch on the quilting line.*

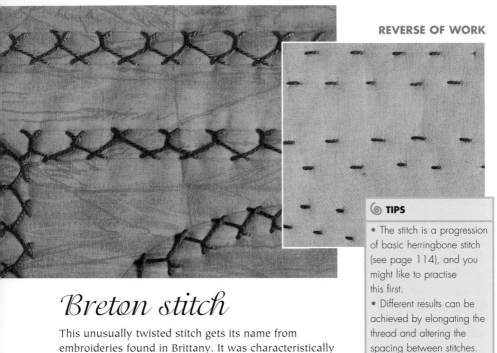

**REVERSE OF WORK**

> **TIPS**
>
> • The stitch is a progression of basic herringbone stitch (see page 114), and you might like to practise this first.
> • Different results can be achieved by elongating the thread and altering the spacing between stitches.

# *Breton stitch*

This unusually twisted stitch gets its name from embroideries found in Brittany. It was characteristically sewn using a blue thread on white fabric, or white thread on blue fabric.

**STEP 1**

Bring the thread out below the quilting line (you will be working horizontally, from left to right). Make a horizontal quilting stitch through all layers, above the quilting line and working from right to left.

**STEP 2**

Pass the needle under the diagonal stitch you have created, from right to left and without catching up the fabric.

**STEP 3**

Make a horizontal quilting stitch below the line, working from right to left. Progress in this way, finishing the thread by taking it into the fabric where it would naturally go for the next stitch.

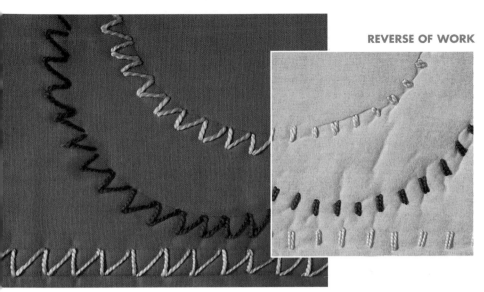

**REVERSE OF WORK**

# Glove stitch

Traditionally, this stitch was used in the making of fine leather gloves. Two stitches are taken into the same place with each repeat, so the back of the work looks heavier than some.

**STEP 1**

*Bring the thread to the surface of the work, on the quilting line. Working horizontally, take the needle in above the line and make a vertical quilting stitch down towards you, bringing the needle out on the line at the original starting point.*

**STEP 2**

*Move along the line and take the needle in above the quilting line once more, stitching vertically and down towards you, bringing the needle up on the line.*

**STEP 3**

*Take the needle in above the line at the same point that it went into previously. Make a vertical quilting stitch down towards you, bringing the needle out on the line at the same point used previously.*

**STEP 4**

*Move along the line and make the next vertical quilting stitch. Continue in this way along the quilting line.*

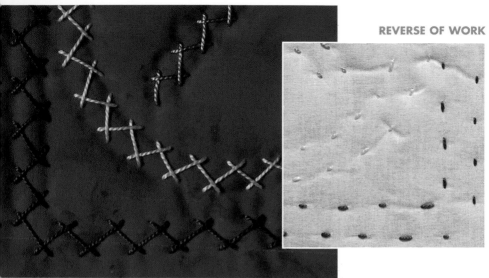

**REVERSE OF WORK**

# *Herringbone stitch*

You can have fun altering the appearance of this stitch by either widening the stitch above and below the line, or elongating or shortening it along the line.

## STEP 1

Bring the thread to the surface of the work, below the quilting line. Move forwards along the quilting line in the direction you want the sewing to go. Take a small, horizontal quilting stitch through all layers, above the line, working backwards.

## STEP 2

Move forwards along the line again. Take a small, horizontal quilting stitch under the line, working backwards.

## STEP 3

Repeat steps 1 and 2 to complete the row.

## STEP 4

To take the herringbone neatly around a corner, make two stitches outside the corner of the quilting line and then carry on as before.

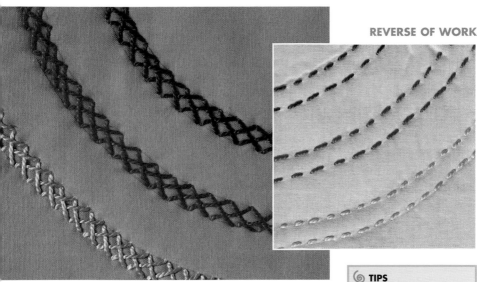

**REVERSE OF WORK**

# Closed herringbone

Closed herringbone stitch is useful when a definite, fairly heavy line of stitching is required for added emphasis.

**TIPS**

- This stitch can be worked wider, but if taken too wide it will distort the fabric.
- The spacing of the stitch will depend on the length of the quilting stitch that is taken above and below the quilting line.

## STEP 1

*Bring the thread to the surface of the work, above the quilting line. Move forwards in the direction you want the sewing to go. Take a small, horizontal quilting stitch through all layers, above the line, working backwards.*

## STEP 2

*Move forwards along the line again. Take a small, horizontal quilting stitch under the line, working backwards.*

## STEP 3

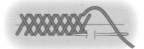

*Repeat steps 1 and 2, making sure that each stitch touches the previous stitch, both above the line and below it.*

**REVERSE OF WORK**

# Double herringbone

Work a row of double herringbone stitch in areas where more definition is required. The spacing can be varied, as can the depth and width of the stitches.

### STEP 1

Bring the thread to the surface of the work, below the quilting line, and work a row of basic herringbone stitch (see page 114).

### STEP 2

Bring the second or contrasting thread out at the beginning of the quilting line, but this time start above the quilting line.

### STEP 3

Move along the row and make a quilting stitch in a backwards direction in the first space provided by the previously sewn herringbone stitches.

### STEP 4

Pass the needle under the next sloping thread (do not catch the fabric) before taking the next quilting stitch above the line, working backwards and between the next two base herringbone stitches. Carry on in this way, working in the spaces provided by the row of herringbone stitch and only passing the needle under a thread on its way upwards (the needle does not go through the fabric).

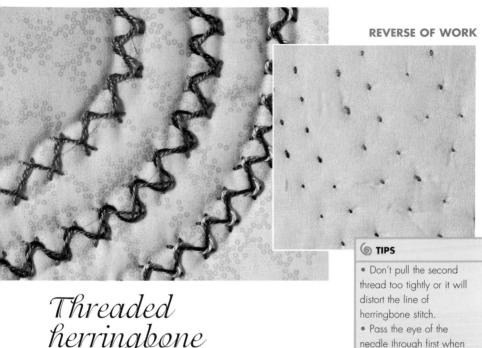

**REVERSE OF WORK**

# Threaded herringbone

When the basic herringbone stitch needs a little more texture and interest, it can be threaded through with a contrasting thread for added emphasis.

> ⓖ **TIPS**
> • Don't pull the second thread too tightly or it will distort the line of herringbone stitch.
> • Pass the eye of the needle through first when threading, or use a blunt tapestry needle.

### STEP 1

Bring the thread to the surface of the work, below the quilting line, and work a row of basic herringbone stitch (see page 114).

### STEP 2

Bring the second or contrasting thread out at the beginning of the quilting line, at the same point that the original herringbone stitch thread began. Pass the needle under the first sloping stitch, from right to left.

### STEP 3

Pass the needle under the next sloping stitch, from right to left. Continue in this way, working along the base row of herringbone stitch. Finish the second or contrasting thread in the same place that you finished the thread of the herringbone stitch.

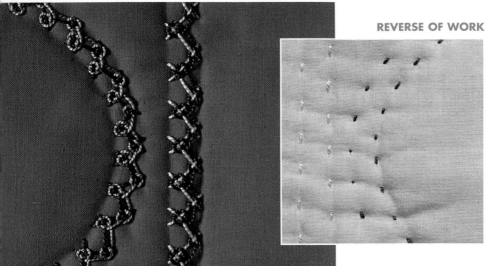

**REVERSE OF WORK**

# *Laced herringbone*

An extremely decorative stitch. The tight loops are less likely to snag than other types of lacing, so it's suitable for items frequently handled, such as a bed quilt.

### STEP 1

*Work a row of herringbone stitch (see page 114) and turn upside down. Bring out the second thread at the beginning of the herringbone row. Starting below the line, work in an anticlockwise direction around the criss-cross part of the base thread: pass the needle from left to right under the first part of the base thread, continue over and under the base thread.*

### STEP 2

*Now take the needle over the next base thread and back under the second thread; over the next sloping thread base thread; under the next base threads. Then move along to the next criss-cross of base thread above the line.*

### STEP 3

*Work in an anticlockwise way around this. Go under, over, under and over the base threads; under the contrast thread, as shown; over, under, over and under the base threads; over the contrast thread and back down to the next criss-cross section below the line.*

### STEP 4

*Go back down to the next criss-cross section below the line, and repeat, as shown.*

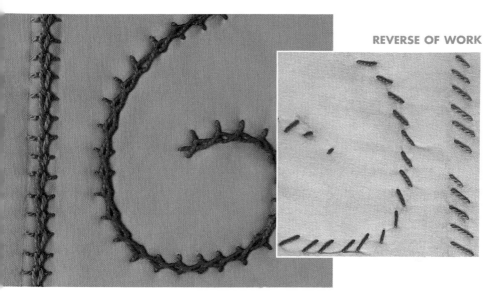

**REVERSE OF WORK**

# Vandyke stitch

Vandyke stitch is attractive and deceptively simple. It has a raised, central chain effect and this will be more pronounced if a thicker thread is used.

### STEP 1

Bring the thread out on the left of the quilting line and a little way down from your starting point. Take the needle back up to the beginning of the quilting line and make a small, horizontal quilting stitch.

### STEP 2

Take the needle in on the right of the line, level with where the thread came out on the left of the line, and make a quilting stitch through all layers, downwards and diagonally across the line, back to the left-hand side.

### STEP 3

Pass the needle behind the two crossed threads that have appeared and pull the thread through.

### STEP 4

Repeat steps 2 and 3, finishing with a step 2 stitch.

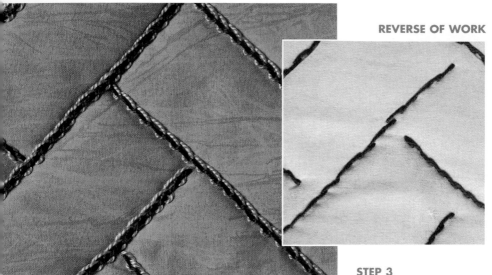

**REVERSE OF WORK**

# Pekinese stitch

An attractive and ornamental stitch with a slightly raised appearance, Pekinese stitch gives the impression of a decorative plait sitting on the surface of the work.

### STEP 1

Bring the thread to the surface of the work, at the beginning of the quilting line. Work a foundation row of basic backstitch (see page 71).

### STEP 2

Bring the second or contrasting thread up at one end of the quilting line, but this time slightly below the line itself. Pass the needle upwards and underneath the second stitch along in the foundation row.

### STEP 3

Return along the foundation row and pass the needle down behind the first stitch of the foundation row, bringing the needle in front of the contrast thread sitting below it.

### STEP 4

Move along two stitches on the foundation row and repeat steps 2 and 3. You are moving two foundation stitches forwards followed by one foundation stitch back each time.

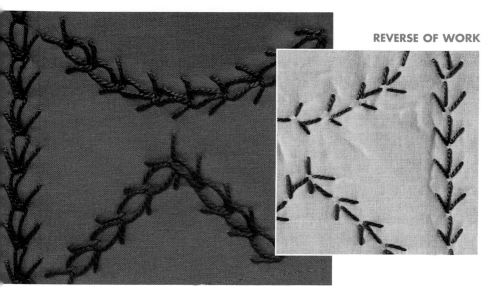

**REVERSE OF WORK**

# Wheatear stitch

This stitch looks similar to an ear of corn. It is constructed from a mixture of quilting stitches and looping stitches.

### STEP 1

*Bring the thread to the surface of the work, on the left of the quilting line. Take the needle into the fabric slightly further down the line and on the line itself. Make a quilting stitch through all the layers, diagonally to the right and upwards.*

### STEP 2

*Take the needle back into the fabric, at the same point where the thread last went in, and make a quilting stitch down towards you, bringing the needle out on the line.*

### STEP 3

*Pass the needle from right to left behind the two stitches of thread that have now appeared.*

### STEP 4

*Take the needle back in on the line, at the same point where the thread last came out, and make a quilting stitch diagonally upwards and out to the left to start again. For subsequent stitches, when you pass the needle behind the two outer "legs" of the previous stitch, bring the needle in front of the central loop at the same time – this will help the stitch to lie flat on the surface of the fabric.*

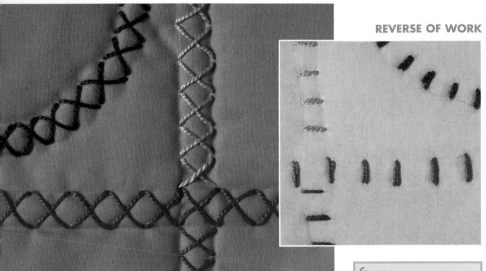

**REVERSE OF WORK**

# Cross stitch

Cross stitch is probably one of the oldest and most recognizable of embroidery stitches, and one not readily associated with quilting. There are many alternative ways to stitch it.

**STEP 1**

Bring the thread to the surface of the work, just below the quilting line. Moving forwards along the line, take the needle in above the line, make a vertical quilting stitch through all the layers and bring the needle out below the line.

**STEP 2**

Return along the foundation row of diagonal stitches to complete the crosses, working in the opposite direction, but still taking a vertical quilting stitch, using the previous exit and entry points for the thread as a guideline.

**◎ TIPS**

• This method maintains a neat appearance on the back of the project.
• It is a good method for closely woven fabric, where you do not have the benefit of an open weave to guide the length and width of the stitches.

**STEP 3**

Continue working along the row until you have covered all the foundation row and changed the diagonal stitches to cross stitches.

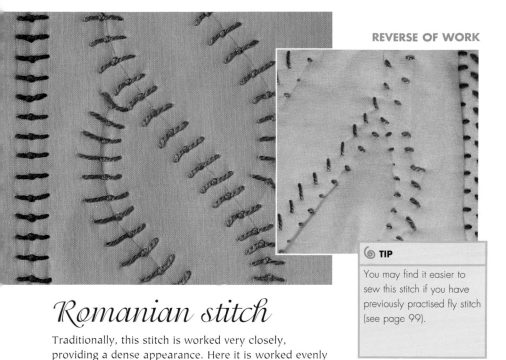

**REVERSE OF WORK**

> **TIP**
>
> You may find it easier to sew this stitch if you have previously practised fly stitch (see page 99).

# Romanian stitch

Traditionally, this stitch is worked very closely, providing a dense appearance. Here it is worked evenly spaced to make it more suitable for quilting projects.

### STEP 1

*Bring the thread to the surface of the work, to the left of the quilting line. Holding the thread down and around to the right, take the needle into the fabric on the right-hand side of the quilting line, level with where the thread began on the left, and make a quilting stitch horizontally, bringing the needle up in the centre and above the waiting thread.*

### STEP 2

*Now take the needle in, below the waiting thread, to secure it. Make a diagonal stitch downwards and out to the left, bringing the needle up level with your original starting point.*

### STEP 3

*Hold the thread down and around to the right, take the needle in on the right-hand side and bring it up in the centre again, above the waiting thread. Repeat this and step 2 to progress along the quilting line. Finish with a small securing stitch in the centre.*

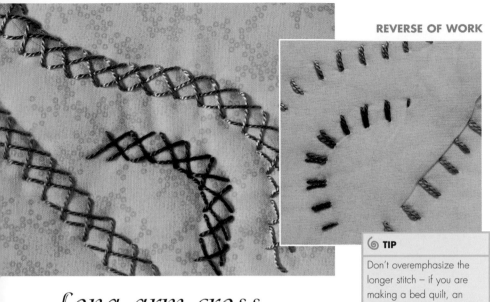

**REVERSE OF WORK**

## 🌀 TIP

Don't overemphasize the longer stitch – if you are making a bed quilt, an overlong stitch may snag and pull.

# Long-arm cross

Often to be found on counted thread work, this stitch is equally useful and easy to sew on closely woven fabric for a quilting pattern.

**STEP 1**

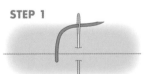

Bring the thread to the surface of the work, below the quilting line. Move forwards along the line (approximately twice the length of the required shorter stitch). Take the needle into the fabric above the line, and make a vertical quilting stitch down towards you through all the layers, bringing the needle out below the line.

**STEP 2**

Bring the needle halfway back along this first stitch, take it in above the line (level with the top of the previous stitch) and, making a vertical quilting stitch, bring the needle out below the line (level with the bottom of the previous stitch).

**STEP 3**

Move forwards along the line, twice the length of the shorter stitch, and make a vertical stitch down towards you again. Repeat steps 2 and 3 and continue working along the quilting line, balancing the spacing of the stitches as evenly as possible. (You will need to adjust the spacing when working this stitch on a curve.)

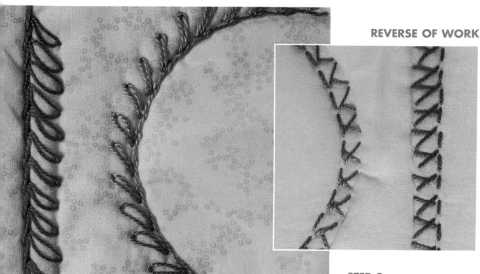

# Petal stitch

The diagonal loops of this stitch give the impression of flower petals blowing in the breeze. It is most effective when used on the outer edge of a curved design.

**STEP 1**

Bring the thread to the surface of the work, a little way forwards along the quilting line. Hold the thread above the work, take the needle back to the beginning of the quilting line and make a short quilting stitch through all the layers, following the line and bringing the needle out underneath the waiting thread.

**STEP 2**

Hold the thread around to the left to form a loop. Take the needle in on the line, underneath the stitch and at the point where the thread last came out of the fabric. Make a quilting stitch diagonally over to the left, bringing the needle out into the waiting loop of thread.

**STEP 3**

Take the needle in under the loop of thread and stitch diagonally upwards and to the left, bringing the needle out on the line and at a length of two stitches away from the previous stitch.

**STEP 4**

Repeat step 1, taking the needle in at the top of the last loop and below the bar stitch sitting on the line.

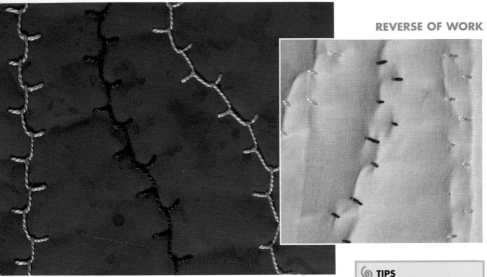

**REVERSE OF WORK**

# Open Cretan

Open Cretan stitch is not usually associated with work on closely woven fabric, but it makes an interesting quilting stitch – a slight variation on herringbone stitch (see page 114).

## TIPS

• Because of the two angles (upwards and downwards) required for the needle, and the need to loop the thread, this stitch is better worked horizontally.
• Use the thumb of your non-sewing hand to place the thread ready for the next stitch.

**STEP 1**

Bring the thread to the surface of the work, at the beginning of the quilting line. Hold the thread over to the left and downwards. Make a small, upwardly vertical quilting stitch through all layers, below the quilting line and into the waiting loop of thread.

**STEP 2**

Hold the thread to the left and upwards. Make a small, downwardly vertical quilting stitch, above the quilting line and into the waiting loop of thread.

**STEP 3**

Repeat steps 1 and 2 as you progress along the quilting line from right to left.

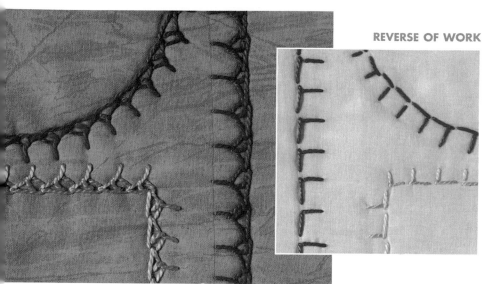

**REVERSE OF WORK**

# *Mountmellick*

Mountmellick stitch was originally to be found on whitework embroidery stitched in Ireland. This unusual and complex stitch is amazingly easy to sew.

**STEP 1**

*Bring the thread to the surface of the work, at the beginning of the quilting line. Move a little way down the quilting line and make a horizontal quilting stitch through all layers, working from right to left and bringing the needle up on the quilting line.*

**STEP 2**

*Pass the needle under the existing stitch (not through the fabric) from right to left.*

**STEP 3**

*Loop the thread to the left and upwards, and take the needle in at the original starting point. Make a quilting stitch forwards along the line, bringing the needle up to meet the last stitch and into the waiting loop of thread.*

**STEP 4**

*Repeat steps 1, 2 and 3, making sure at step 3 that the needle is taken into the chain of the previous thread. Progress along the quilting line and finish with a small securing stitch outside the last complete Mountmellick stitch.*

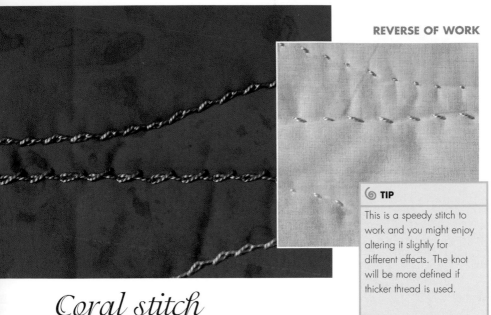

**REVERSE OF WORK**

# *Coral stitch*

The final appearance of a row of coral stitch depends on the spacing of the stitches, and the sharpness and length of the diagonal stitch that is taken through all the layers.

### STEP 1

*Work horizontally and from right to left. Bring the thread to the surface of the work, at the beginning of the quilting line. Hold the thread ahead of the work, along the line and looped down and around to the right. Make a shallow, diagonal quilting stitch through all layers, in above the waiting thread and the quilting line, bringing the needle out below the waiting thread, below the quilting line and into the waiting loop of thread.*

### STEP 2

*Hold the thread forwards along the line again. Make a second quilting stitch, in above the thread and the line, and out below the thread and the line, into the waiting loop of thread.*

### STEP 3

*Continue in this way, finishing the thread outside a knot or loop.*

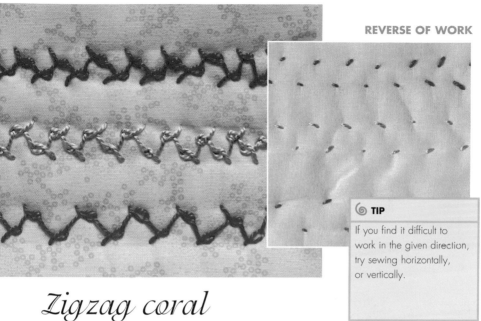

**REVERSE OF WORK**

> **TIP**
>
> If you find it difficult to work in the given direction, try sewing horizontally, or vertically.

# Zigzag coral

This is a wide stitch, good for areas of a design that need more of a "space-filling" stitch. It can take a little while to get used to the different angles required for the needle.

## STEP 1

*Bring the thread to the surface of the work, above the quilting line. Working from right to left, hold the thread forwards along the line and down and around. Make a diagonal quilting stitch through all layers, in above the thread, forwards and down towards the line, bringing the needle out below the thread and into the waiting loop of thread.*

## STEP 2

*Hold the thread forwards and upwards this time. Make a diagonal quilting stitch, taking the needle in to the right of the thread, stitching forwards and up towards the line, bringing the needle out on the left of the thread and into the waiting loop of thread.*

## STEP 3

*Continue in this way, finishing with the thread outside either the top or bottom coral stitch to secure it.*

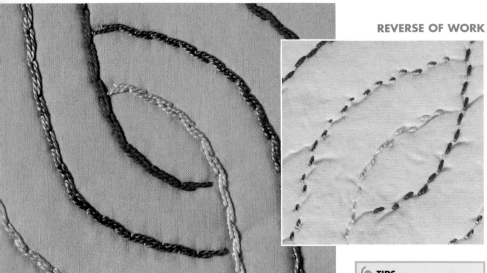

**REVERSE OF WORK**

# Cable stitch

This narrow, solidly defined stitch is very versatile and ideal for stitching continuous line quilting designs and for contour-quilting (outlining) motif patterns.

**STEP 1**

Bring the thread to the surface of the work, at the beginning of the quilting line. Working horizontally, hold the thread below the line and move forwards along the line – make a small horizontal quilting stitch backwards, either on the line or just below it.

**STEP 2**

Hold the thread above the work now and, moving along the line, make a small horizontal stitch backwards, either on the line or just above it, making sure that it touches the previous stitch.

## 🌀 TIPS

• Make sure the stitches are fitted snugly together and worked very close to the quilting line, if not directly on it.
• Alter the appearance of the stitch by shortening or lengthening the individual quilting stitches taken.

**STEP 3**

Repeat steps 1 and 2 to progress along the quilting line.

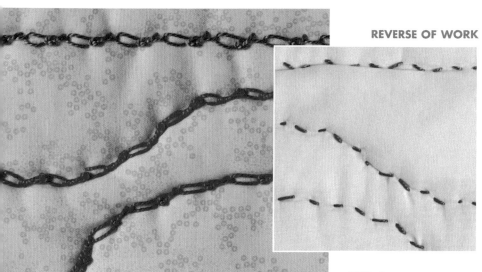

**REVERSE OF WORK**

# Knotted cable chain

This combination of chain stitch and coral stitch includes a knot worked within each chain loop. It is quite simple to sew – the little knots hold the links of the chain in place.

### STEP 1

*Bring the thread out to the surface of the work, at the beginning of the quilting line. Working horizontally, take a small, vertical quilting stitch, in above the line and out below the line, wrapping the thread forwards, around and under the needle. Pull the thread through.*

### STEP 2

*Pass the needle upwards and under the previous stitch that has been sewn (not passing through the fabric).*

### STEP 3

*Use the thumb of your non-sewing hand to hold the thread forwards to form a loop. Take the needle in under the knot and forwards along the line, through all layers, to sew a chain stitch.*

### STEP 4

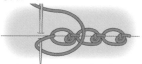

*Make the next vertical quilting stitch, wrapping the thread forwards, around and under the needle and repeating steps 2 and 3.*

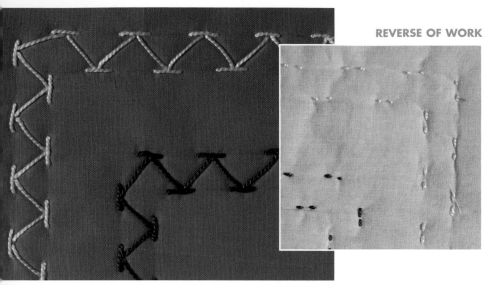

**REVERSE OF WORK**

# Chevron stitch

This stitch can be elongated or shortened, widened or narrowed to suit the desired finished result. It works well on gentle curves and corners.

## STEP 1

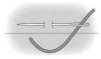

*Bring the thread to the surface of the work, below the quilting line. Move forwards along the line and make a horizontal quilting stitch through all layers, working backwards.*

## STEP 2

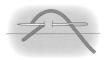

*Hold the thread above the work and make another backwards quilting stitch in front of the previous horizontal stitch. These two stitches form one horizontal bar above the line.*

## STEP 3

*Move forwards along the line and make a horizontal stitch backwards below the line. Hold the thread below the work and make another horizontal stitch backwards below the line, in front of the previous horizontal quilting stitch. These two stitches form one horizontal bar below the line.*

## STEP 4

*Repeat steps 1, 2 and 3 to continue along the line. Finish the thread after completing one full bar either above or below the line.*

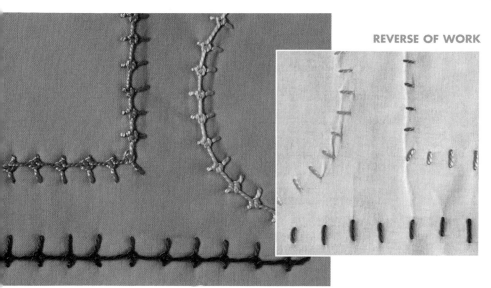

**REVERSE OF WORK**

# Double knot

A narrow stitch, ideal for continuous line quilting designs and for contour-quilting motif patterns. It has a slightly raised effect with intermittent knots.

## STEP 1

Bring the thread to the surface of the work, at the beginning of the quilting line. Move forwards along the line and make a vertical quilting stitch through all layers, taking the needle in above the line and bringing it out below the line. Pull the thread through.

## STEP 2

Hold the thread forwards and above the work and pass the needle under the previous stitch made (not through the fabric). Pull the thread through.

## STEP 3

Use the thumb of your non-sewing hand to hold the thread forwards and above the work. Pass the needle under the top bar of the previous stitch, bringing the needle over the lower bar and into the waiting loop of thread. Pull the thread through to form the double knot.

## STEP 4

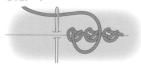

Move along the quilting line to make the next quilting stitch and repeat steps 1, 2 and 3 to form a row of double knot stitch. Finish the thread outside the last double knot sewn.

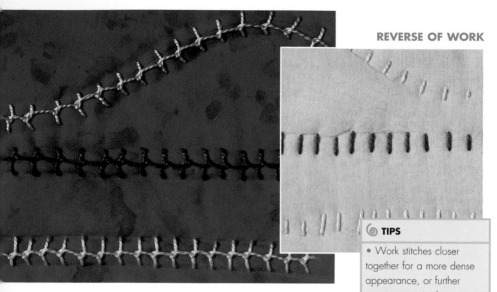

**REVERSE OF WORK**

# *Loop stitch*

Loop stitch is a wide stitch made up from one quilting stitch and one looping stitch, with a slightly raised centre. It is an easy stitch to sew fluidly and speedily.

> ⑥ **TIPS**
>
> • Work stitches closer together for a more dense appearance, or further apart as required.
> • Pass the eye of the needle under the previous stitches, rather than the point, to avoid catching unwanted fibres or thread.

**STEP 1**

*Bring the thread to the surface of the work, at the beginning of the quilting line. Move forwards along the quilting line and make a vertical quilting stitch through all layers, taking the needle in above the line and bringing it out below the line. Pull the thread through.*

**STEP 2**

*Use the thumb of your non-sewing hand to hold the thread forwards and pass the needle under the previous stitch made and over the waiting thread in front of it (it does not pass through the fabric). Pull the thread through.*

**STEP 3**

*Move along the quilting line and make the next vertical quilting stitch, repeating steps 1 and 2 to create a row of loop stitches. Finish the thread after a looping stage.*

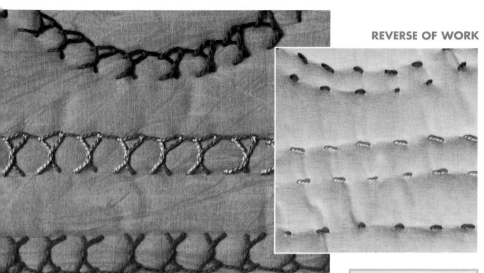

**REVERSE OF WORK**

# *Bonnet stitch*

Bonnet stitch is a wide stitch with a complex twisted appearance on the surface of the work, but with neat, parallel rows of running stitch on the back.

## TIPS

Alter the final appearance of the stitch by changing the spacing between each stitch and also the width at which it is sewn.

### STEP 1

*Bring the thread to the surface of the work, below the quilting line. Working from right to left, hold the thread forwards along the line, upwards and around to form a loop. Make a small, horizontal quilting stitch above the line through all the layers, bringing the needle into the waiting loop of thread.*

### STEP 2

*Now hold the thread forwards and downwards. Make a small, diagonal quilting stitch below the line and downwards, taking the needle in front of the previous thread and into the waiting loop of thread. The centre of the stitch will twist during this process.*

### STEP 3

*Hold the thread forwards and above the line again and, moving forwards along the line, make the next horizontal quilting stitch above the line. Repeat steps 2 and 3 to progress along the quilting line, securing the thread after a diagonal stitch below the line.*

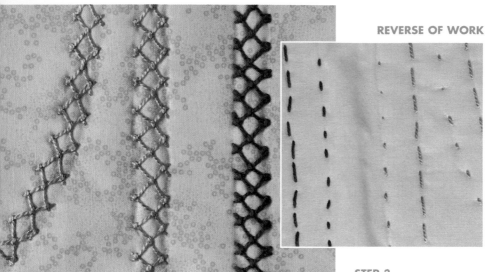

# *Diamond stitch*

This is one of the wider stitches available for quilting.

### STEP 3

*Take the needle into the fabric directly underneath the left-hand* knot and make a longer, vertical quilting stitch downwards.

### STEP 1

*Bring the thread out on the left of the quilting line. Make a short, vertical quilting stitch to the right of the quilting line. Pass the needle behind the stitch that you have just created and hold the thread over the needle to the left and then under the needle to the right before pulling the thread through to form a knot.*

### STEP 2

*Take the needle to the left-hand side of the quilting line. Pass the needle behind the previous stitch and hold the thread over the needle to the left and under the needle to the right before pulling through to form a knot.*

### STEP 4

Take the needle behind the horizontal thread lying across the quilting line and wrap the

thread over the needle to the right and under the needle to the left. Pull through to form a knot.

# Hand-quilting Filling Stitches

Filling stitches can be used to add textural interest to areas of quilting designs that would otherwise remain unquilted and may also look uninteresting.

These stitches can also be used to replace formal quilting designs – entire areas of a quilt can be covered with filling stitches worked in a stylistic and freehand way.

If the appearance of the quilt stitches on the back of your quilt is important for your project, try using a printed fabric rather than a plain fabric for the backing. This will help you relax your stitching.

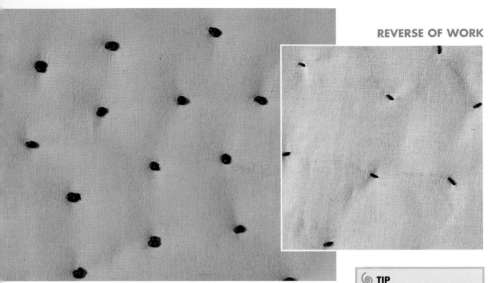

**REVERSE OF WORK**

# Colonial knot

The colonial knot is also known as a candlewicking knot. It is very similar in appearance to the French knot (see page 140), but is slightly larger and sits higher.

**⊚ TIP**

These knots are commonly stitched close together to form a continuous line, but also make a versatile alternative knot for a hand-quilting filling stitch.

**STEP 1**

*Bring the thread to the surface of the work. Hold the thread over the needle to the right and under the needle to the left; and back over the needle point to the right and under the needle point to the left.*

**STEP 2**

*Pull the thread taut to stabilize the knot while you take the needle into the fabric through all layers, just to one side of where the thread initially came out.*

**STEP 3**

*If you are working several knots within a short space of each other, use the stitch to quilt through all layers of the project. Make a small quilting stitch on the back of the work, then take the point of the needle into the wadding and travel through the wadding to the area for the next knot.*

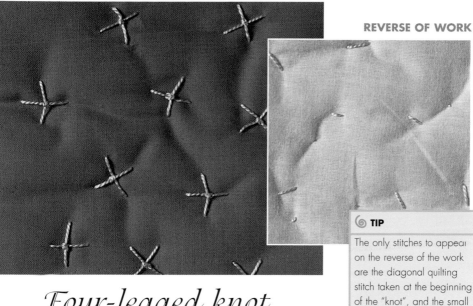

**REVERSE OF WORK**

# *Four-legged knot*

The four-legged knot is an attractive knot, which resembles an upright cross stitch with a textural knot in the centre.

> **TIP**
>
> The only stitches to appear on the reverse of the work are the diagonal quilting stitch taken at the beginning of the "knot", and the small quilting stitch that secures the stitch and moves you to the area for the next stitch.

**STEP 1**

Bring the thread to the surface of the work. Hold the thread down vertically and make a diagonal stitch upwards and out to the right.

**STEP 2**

Hold the thread across the vertical stitch and loop it downwards. Pass the needle behind both of these crossed threads, at a diagonal downwards and into the waiting loop of thread. Pull through to form a central knot.

**STEP 3**

Take the needle out to the left of the four-legged knot to complete it. If working several knots within a short space of each other, use this last stitch to quilt through the layers of the project. Make a small quilting stitch through to the back of the work, then take the point of the needle into the wadding and travel through the wadding to the area for the next knot.

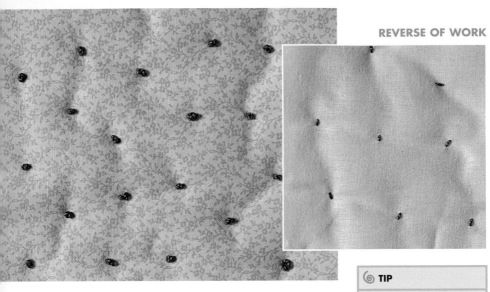

**REVERSE OF WORK**

# French knot

When making the French knot, the thread is wrapped around the needle before it enters the fabric. Make one or two wraps of the needle, according to the preferred size of knot.

> ⑥ **TIP**
>
> For a chunkier knot, use a thicker thread to give more definition to the end result.

### STEP 1

*Bring the thread to the surface of the work. Hold the needle in your sewing hand and wrap the thread forwards over the needle and back towards you under the needle (for a chunkier knot, repeat once more).*

### STEP 2

*Hold the thread taut so the wrapped thread stays firm while you take the needle back into the fabric close to where the thread initially emerged.*

### STEP 3

*If working several knots within a short space of each other, use this last stitch to quilt through the layers of your project. Make a small quilting stitch through to the back of the work, then take the point of the needle into the wadding and travel through the wadding to the area for the next knot.*

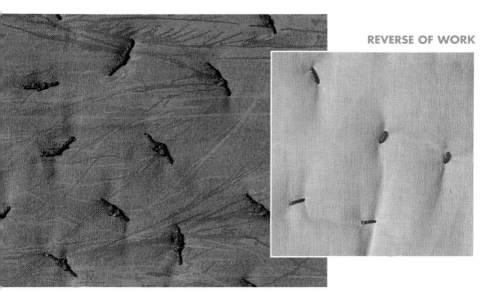

**REVERSE OF WORK**

# Danish knot

This stitch looks like a chunky knot on a long bar. The knot is formed by wrapping the thread under the existing bar stitch without catching the fabric.

**STEP 1**

Bring the thread to the surface of the work. Take the needle in any direction and make a quilting stitch back to the centre of the previous stitch, bringing the needle up to the left-hand side of the thread.

**STEP 2**

Hold the thread down and around to the right, and pass the needle under the long bar stitch without catching up any fabric. Pull the thread through.

**STEP 3**

Hold the thread down and around to the right again. Pass the needle under the long bar stitch, below the previous wrap and bring the needle into the waiting loop of thread. Pull the thread through to form a knot.

**STEP 4**

Take the thread into the fabric close to the knot to secure it. If working several knots within a short space of each other, use this last stitch to quilt through the layers of the project. Make a small quilting stitch through to the back of the work, then take the point of the needle into the wadding and travel through the wadding to the area for the next knot.

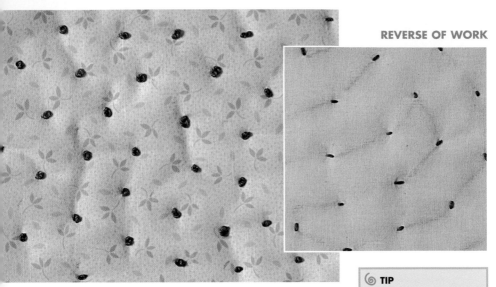

**REVERSE OF WORK**

# Chinese knot

Chinese knots are also known as Pekin knots or forbidden knots. They can be found in antique embroideries throughout China.

> 🌀 **TIP**
>
> Similar in appearance to a French knot, but with a slightly different shape. It also tends to sit flatter on the surface of the fabric.

### STEP 1

*Bring the thread to the surface of the work. Loop the thread down and around to the left to form a clockwise circle. Using your non-sewing hand, lift this loop up and over on itself so that it forms a circle travelling antclockwise.*

### STEP 2

*Support the loop of thread with your non-sewing thumb, take the needle into the fabric inside the loop and make a stitch to secure it.*

### STEP 3

*If working several knots within a short space of each other, use this last stitch to quilt through the layers of the project. Make a small quilting stitch to the back of the work, then take the point of the needle into the wadding and travel through the wadding to the area for the next knot.*

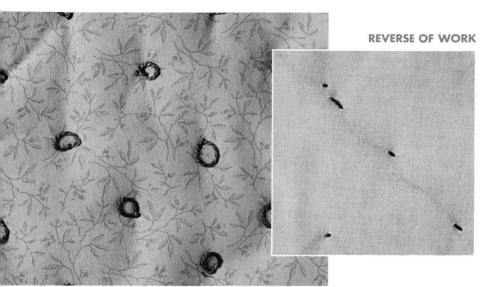

**REVERSE OF WORK**

# *Looped Chinese knot*

Practise the Chinese knot (see page 142) before trying this variation, which features an additional decorative loop. Make the loop as small or as large as you prefer.

**STEP 1**

*Bring the thread to the surface of the work. Loop the thread down and around to the left to form a clockwise circle. Using your non-sewing hand, lift this loop up and over on itself so that it forms a circle travelling anticlockwise.*

**STEP 2**

*Support the loop of thread with your non-sewing thumb, while taking the needle into the fabric inside the loop.*

**STEP 3**

*Keep hold of the loop so it doesn't disappear as the needle is taken into the fabric. Once the thread and the knot are pulled taut, the loop will sit on the surface of the work.*

**STEP 4**

*If working several knots within a short space of each other, use this last stitch to quilt through the layers of the project. Make a small quilting stitch to the back of the work, then take the point of the needle into the wadding and travel through the wadding to the area for the next knot.*

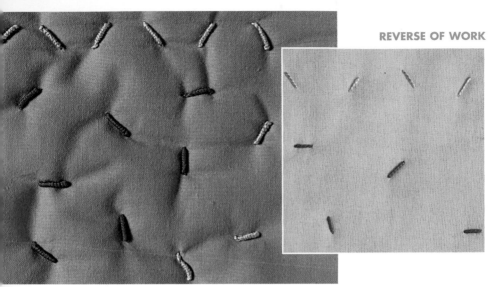

**REVERSE OF WORK**

# *Bullion knot*

The thread is wrapped several times around the core thread to form each stitch. Bullion knot can be worked to whatever length you prefer.

**STEP 1**

*Bring the thread to the surface of the work. Take the needle into the fabric and make a quilting stitch through all layers, working towards your starting point. Bring the needle up through the fabric close to where it first emerged, but do not pull it through at this point.*

**STEP 2**

*Hold the needle and, using your other hand, firmly wrap the thread around the shank of the needle several times – as many times as required to fill the length of the stitch.*

**STEP 3**

*Hold the wrapping threads very securely while you pull the needle through.*

**STEP 4**

*To secure the knot, take the needle back into the same place as used for making the first stitch. If working several knots within a short space of each other, use this last stitch to bridge through the wadding to the next area.*

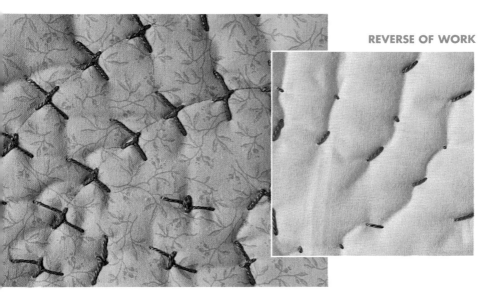

**REVERSE OF WORK**

# *Sword-edge stitch*

This stitch can be sewn in a line for continuous line quilting designs, or used as a filling stitch, scattered across your work. The length and width can be varied.

**STEP 4**

**STEP 1**

*Bring the thread to the surface of the work. Take the needle in below and slightly to the left of the starting point. Make a quilting stitch diagonally up and to the left, through all layers, and pull the thread through.*

**STEP 2**

*Pass the needle upwards, or from right to left, under the existing diagonal stitch.*

**STEP 3**

*Take the needle in directly above the lower leg of the sword-edge stitch to secure it.*

*If working several scattered stitches within a short space of each other, use this last stitch to quilt through the layers of the project. Make a small quilting stitch through to the back of the work, then take the point of the needle into the wadding and travel through the wadding to the area for the next knot.*

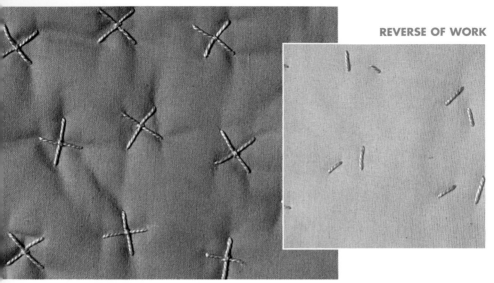

**REVERSE OF WORK**

# Tied cross

This makes an interesting filling stitch when scattered over a quilt project. It is possible to vary the size of the cross stitch legs, but they should remain even.

**STEP 1**

*Take the needle into the fabric a short distance away. Make a quilting stitch through all the layers, vertically and upwards, bringing the needle out level with where the thread first emerged.*

**STEP 2**

*Carry the thread across the existing stitch just produced. Take the needle into the fabric level with the upper leg of the stitch, working diagonally towards the centre of the cross, bringing the needle up to one side of it.*

**STEP 3**

*Take the needle down on the opposite side of the cross, close to the existing threads, to secure it.*

**STEP 4**

*If working several scattered stitches within a short space of each other, use this last stitch to quilt through the layers of the project. Make a small quilting stitch through to the back of the work, then take the point of the needle into the wadding and travel through the wadding to the area for the next stitch.*

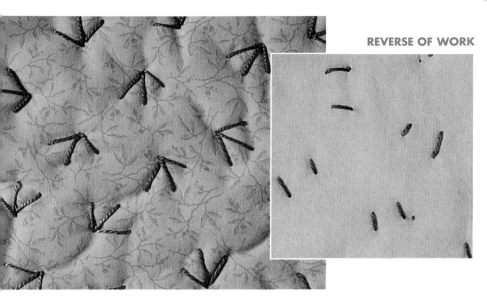

**REVERSE OF WORK**

# Detached fern

Detached fern stitches can be scattered at random and positioned in different directions across a quilt project, providing a pretty foliage effect.

**STEP 1**

*Bring the thread to the surface of the work. Take the needle out to the right and make a quilting stitch through all layers, stitching diagonally to the left and slightly upwards. Pull the thread through.*

**STEP 2**

*Take the needle in at the place where the thread first emerged and make a quilting stitch diagonally to the left and slightly upwards.*

**STEP 3**

*Take the needle back into the fabric at your initial starting point to secure the stitch.*

**STEP 4**

*If working several scattered stitches within a short space of each other, use this last stitch to quilt through the layers of the project. Make a small quilting stitch through to the back of the work, then take the point of the needle into the wadding and travel through the wadding to the area for the next stitch.*

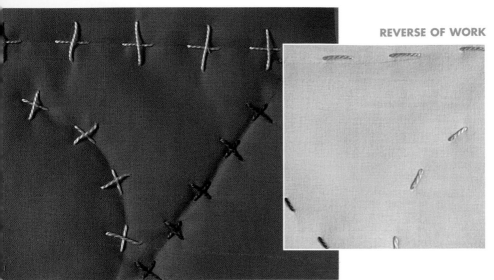

**REVERSE OF WORK**

# *Upright cross*

Upright cross stitch is a variation of basic cross stitch (see page 122) and a looser variation of tied cross stitch (see page 146). The two stitches are not linked or looped together.

**STEP 3**

*If working several scattered stitches within a short space of each other, sew one horizontal bar stitch and then cross it over with a second stitch running at right angles to the first stitch. Use the last stitch to quilt through the layers of the project. Make a small quilting stitch through to the back of the work, taking the point of the needle into the wadding and travelling through the wadding to the area for the next stitch.*

**STEP 1**

*Bring the thread to the surface of the work and work a line of basic running stitch (see page 67).*

**STEP 2**

*Turn your work and, starting at the beginning of the row, take the needle in above each horizontal stitch, centrally, and out below the next horizontal stitch, centrally. Do not work these stitches through all layers – pass the needle through the top fabric and the wadding only.*

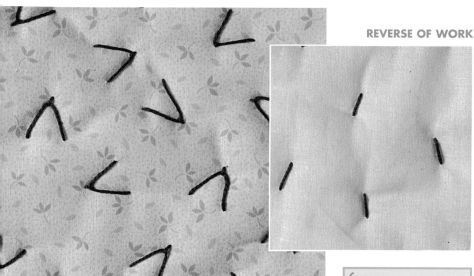

**REVERSE OF WORK**

# Detached fly

Detached fly stitch makes a wonderfully quick and simple filling stitch, adding movement to your quilt work.

> ⊚ **TIPS**
>
> • While sewing the V-shape, one quilting stitch is taken through all the layers of the work.
> • The securing stitch at the bottom point of the "V" can be run into the top fabric and the wadding only.

### STEP 1

*Bring the thread to the surface of the work. Hold the thread downwards and around to the right. Make a quilting stitch through all layers, working diagonally downwards and slightly to the left, bringing the needle into the waiting loop of thread.*

### STEP 2

*Make a quilting stitch to secure the detached fly stitch.*

### STEP 3

*If working several scattered stitches within a short space of each other, use the last stitch to quilt through the layers of the project. Make a small quilting stitch through to the back of the work, taking the point of the needle into the wadding and travelling through the wadding to the area for the next stitch.*

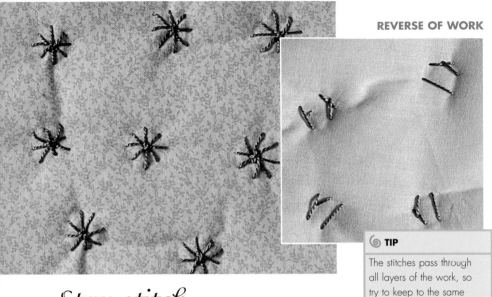

**REVERSE OF WORK**

# Star stitch

Star stitch is a decorative filling stitch, adding both texture and interest to quilt work. The cross stitches may be worked in different colours.

**STEP 1**

Bring the thread to the surface of the work and, working through all layers, work a large and upright cross stitch by placing two diagonal stitches, one on top of the other.

**STEP 2**

Work an equal-sized diagonal cross stitch on top of the previous upright cross stitch, ensuring that the legs of the second cross stitch sit evenly between those of the first stitch.

**STEP 3**

Finish by working a tiny cross stitch centrally over all the previous stitches, in order to secure them. If working several scattered stitches within a short space of each other, use the last stitch to quilt through the layers of the project. Make a small quilting stitch through to the back of the work, taking the point of the needle into the wadding and travelling through the wadding to the area for the next stitch.

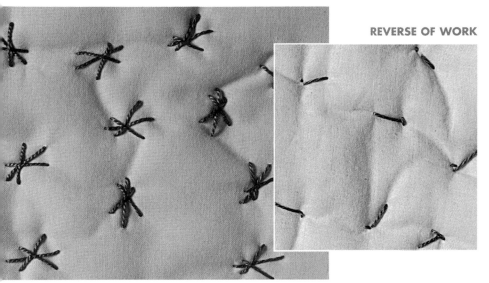

**REVERSE OF WORK**

# *Ermine stitch*

Ermine stitch is a very versatile stitch, which can be worked in formal rows and lines, as well as used for filling areas to give added texture and interest.

**STEP 1**

Bring the thread to the surface of the work. Take the needle into the fabric vertically beneath your starting point, and make a quilting stitch through all layers diagonally upwards and to the left of the previous stitch. Pull the thread through.

**STEP 2**

Take the needle in to the right of the first vertical stitch and just a short way up from the bottom of this stitch. Make a short, horizontal quilting stitch, bringing the needle up to the left of the first vertical stitch.

**STEP 3**

Carrying the thread across the previous two stitches, take the needle in on the right of the first vertical stitch, level with the left-hand branch, to secure this stitch. If working several scattered stitches within a short space of each other, use the last stitch to quilt through the layers of the project. Make a small quilting stitch through to the back of the work, taking the point of the needle into the wadding and travelling through the wadding to the area for the next stitch.

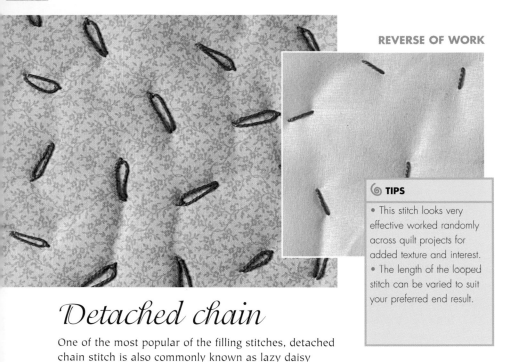

**⑥ TIPS**

• This stitch looks very effective worked randomly across quilt projects for added texture and interest.
• The length of the looped stitch can be varied to suit your preferred end result.

# Detached chain

One of the most popular of the filling stitches, detached chain stitch is also commonly known as lazy daisy stitch. It is often used to sew flowers and leaves.

## STEP 1

*Bring the thread to the surface of the work. Hold the thread forwards, ahead of your work and looped around. Take the needle back into the fabric where the thread first emerged (or very close to it) and make a quilting stitch forwards through all layers, bringing the needle up into the waiting loop of thread. Pull the thread through.*

## STEP 2

*Make a quilting stitch to secure the looped stitch.*

## STEP 3

*If working several scattered stitches within a short space of each other, use the last stitch to quilt through the layers of the project. Make a small quilting stitch through to the back of the work, taking the point of the needle into the wadding and travelling through the wadding to the area for the next stitch.*

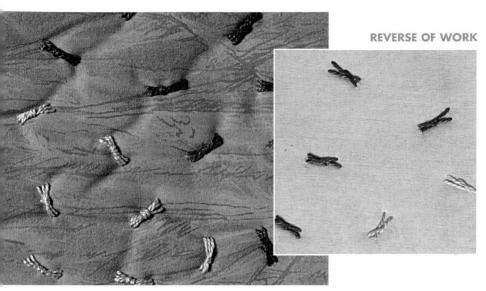

**REVERSE OF WORK**

# *Sheaf stitch*

Sheaf stitch is a combination of three parallel stitches that are then tied in the centre with a loop of thread and bear a resemblance to a sheaf of wheat.

**STEP 3**

*Take the needle into the fabric to complete the three vertical stitches and bring it out to the left, halfway up the three stitches.*

**STEP 1**

*Bring the thread to the surface of the work and work a vertical quilting stitch through all layers. Bring the needle back out close to your original starting point and just to the right of it.*

**STEP 4**

*Pass the needle twice around the three stitches without catching up any fabric, pulling the thread in firmly to clinch them in their centre. Make a quilting stitch to secure this complete sheaf stitch. If working several scattered stitches within a short space of each other, use the last stitch to quilt through the layers of the project. Make a small quilting stitch through to the back of the work, taking the point of the needle into the wadding and travelling through the wadding to the area for the next stitch.*

**STEP 2**

*Work a second vertical stitch, bringing the needle up alongside your original starting point, but this time on the opposite side.*

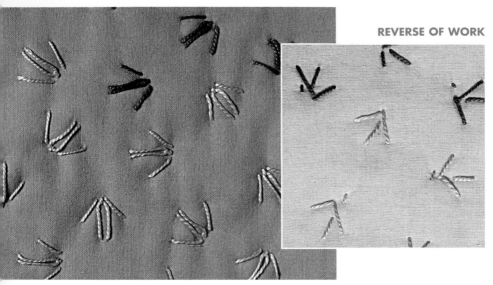

**REVERSE OF WORK**

# Tête de boeuf

Tête de boeuf stitch produces a very attractive filling stitch. The name means "bull's head" – you can see the "bull's horns" on either side of the "head."

### STEP 1

*Holding the thread forwards and round and taking the needle into the fabric close to the starting point, make a quilting stitch. Bring the needle up a short distance away and into the waiting loop of thread.*

### STEP 2

*Take the needle into the fabric underneath the loop that you have made and make a diagonal quilting stitch, upwards and out to the left of the loop.*

### STEP 3

*Take the needle into the fabric just below and to the left of the centre of the loop stitch. Stitch diagonally upwards and out to the right of the loop stitch.*

### STEP 4

*Take the thread back into the fabric, to the bottom right of the central loop, to secure it. If working several scattered stitches within a short space of each other, use the last stitch to quilt through the layers of the project. Make a small quilting stitch through to the back of the work, taking the point of the needle into the wadding and travelling through the wadding to the area for the next stitch.*

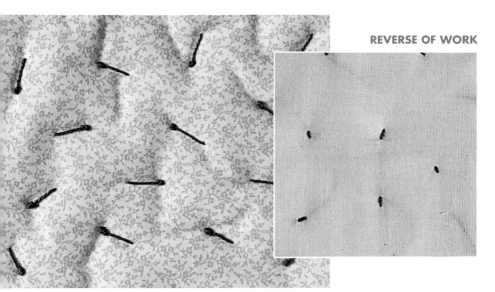

# Pistil stitch

Pistil stitch is a very narrow and delicate filling stitch, comprised of a long bar stitch with a French knot sewn at the end for added textural interest.

## STEP 1

*Bring the thread to the surface of the work. Holding the thread firmly with your non-sewing hand and keeping the needle a short distance away from the fabric, wrap the thread over the top of the needle to the right and under the point of the needle to the left. Repeat at least twice, but make more wraps if you want a larger knot.*

## STEP 2

*Still holding the thread taut, turn the point of the needle into the fabric, through all the layers. Push the wrapped threads down the needle and onto the surface of the fabric.*

## STEP 3

*Hold the threads firmly with your non-sewing thumb while you take the needle through the fabric to make a quilting stitch. If working several scattered stitches within a short space of each other, after making the small quilting stitch through to the back of the work, take the point of the needle into the wadding and travel through the wadding to the area for the next stitch.*

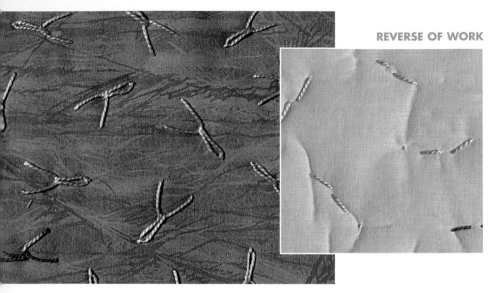

**REVERSE OF WORK**

# Detached wheatear

This stitch is constructed from two looped and secured stitches only. It makes a decorative filling stitch, scattered randomly for added texture and interest.

## STEP 1

*Hold the thread forwards and downwards and take the needle in on the right of your starting point, level with where the thread originally emerged. Make a quilting stitch through all layers, diagonally downwards and over to the left, bringing the needle up into the waiting loop of thread and at a central point between the two upper parts of the stitch.*

## STEP 2

*Hold the thread down and around to the right, take the needle back into the previous V-shaped stitch, close to where the thread came out of the fabric and make a vertical stitch downwards, bringing the needle into the waiting loop of thread.*

## STEP 3

*Make a quilting stitch outside the last loop to secure it. If working several scattered stitches within a short space of each other, use the last stitch to quilt through the layers of the project. Make a small quilting stitch through to the back of the work, taking the point of the needle into the wadding and travelling through the wadding to the area for the next stitch.*

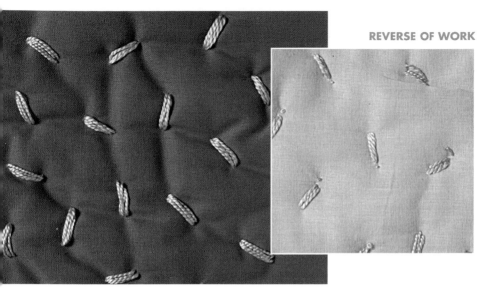

# Granitos stitch

Each granitos stitch is worked through only two holes in the fabric, which helps to plump up the stitch for a textural result.

## STEP 1

Taking the needle in a workable distance above your starting point, make a vertical quilting stitch down and towards you, bringing the needle out into the same hole that the thread first came out of. Pull through.

## STEP 2

Holding the thread over to the left of the first stitch, make a second quilting stitch, working vertically down towards you and using the same two holes as before.

## STEP 3

Hold the thread over to the right of the previous stitches and make a third vertical quilting stitch, using the same two holes to work through. Ensure that the thread sits to the right of the previous stitches.

## STEP 4

Work a fourth stitch to the left of the previous stitches. Make a quilting stitch to secure the completed granitos stitch. If working several scattered stitches within a short space of each other, use the last stitch to bridge through the wadding to the next area.

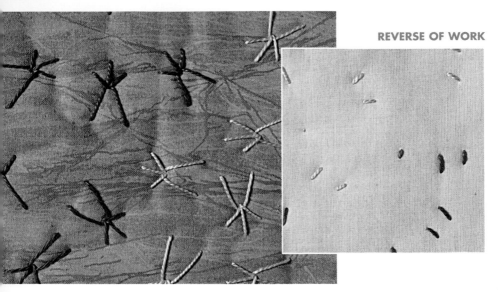

**REVERSE OF WORK**

# Crown stitch

When used as a randomly placed filling stitch, it is not important which way up crown stitch is sitting – the diagrams show the easiest way to sew this stitch.

## STEP 1

Bring the thread to the surface of the work and work a basic fern stitch (see page 103) through all layers, ensuring that the two side branches of the fern are slightly lower or shorter than the central one. End the completed fern stitch by taking the needle in at the same point as the previous threads, and bringing it out diagonally downwards and to the right-hand side of the work.

## STEP 2

Pass the needle behind all three stitches, making sure that you do not catch up any fabric, and take the needle into the fabric on the left-hand side of the work, level with the right-hand stitch. Use a quilting stitch at this point to secure the completed crown stitch.

## STEP 3

If working several scattered stitches within a short space of each other, use the last stitch as a small quilting stitch carried through to the back of the work. Take the point of the needle into the wadding and travel through the wadding to the area for the next crown stitch. This helps to keep the reverse of the work as neat as possible.

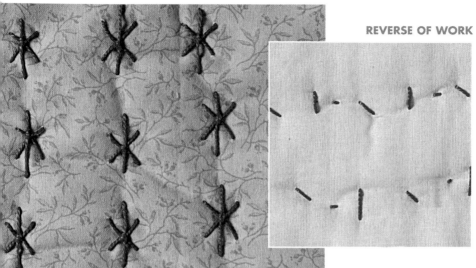

**REVERSE OF WORK**

# Cross and twist

Cross and twist stitch is a wide stitch with a star-like appearance. A looped thread is knotted around the centre, raising the stitch and adding textural interest.

**STEP 1**

*Work a basic cross stitch (see page 122) through all layers. End this stitch by taking the needle upwards and bring it out centrally above the top of the cross stitch.*

**STEP 2**

*Hold the thread down the centre of the cross stitch with your non-sewing thumb. Take the needle in from the left of this thread, behind the cross stitch legs (without catching up any fabric) and out to the right of the waiting thread. Make sure that the waiting thread wraps itself behind the point of the needle from left to right.*

**STEP 3**

*Secure the completed cross and twist stitch by making a quilting stitch centrally below (and further down from) the lower legs of the base cross stitch.*

**STEP 4**

*If working several scattered stitches within a short space of each other, use the last stitch to bridge through the wadding to the next area.*

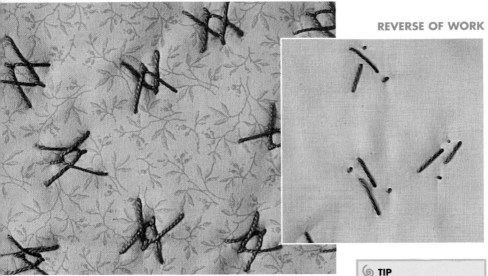

# *Reversed fly*

This intriguing combination of two fly stitches is simple to work. One fly stitch is sewn first, and then a second one is placed on top and upside down.

> **⊚ TIP**
>
> Try to ensure the two overlapping fly stitches are of the same length and width as each other.

### STEP 1

*Sew a basic fly stitch (see page 99) through all layers. End this first fly stitch by bringing the needle out to the bottom left-hand side, slightly lower than the level of the fly stitch.*

### STEP 2

*Hold the thread forwards and to the right. Take the needle in on the right of the fly stitch and make a quilting stitch upwards at an inwards diagonal, emerging centrally within the fly stitch and bringing the needle into the waiting loop of thread. Secure this inverted V-shape with a quilting stitch above it.*

### STEP 3

*If working several scattered stitches within a short space of each other, use the last stitch as a small quilting stitch carried through to the back of the work.*

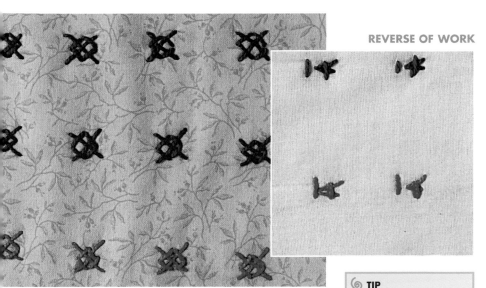

# Square boss

Square boss stitch is a little more formal than some of the available filling stitches. You might like to make a feature of the geometric shape by aligning the stitches in rows.

> **◎ TIP**
>
> If working in rows, achieve extra movement by working stitches randomly and at different angles.

### STEP 1

Work a basic cross stitch (see page 122) through all layers. Make a quilting stitch bringing the needle out at the bottom of the cross stitch, a little higher up than the two lower branches.

### STEP 2

Take the needle in on the right of the stitch and between the two right-hand branches, bringing it out on the left and between the left-hand branches.

### STEP 3

Take the needle back in at the bottom and stitch vertically upwards to exit between the top branches. Follow this with a stitch from right to left, and then finish with a stitch in at the top again to secure the complete square boss stitch. If working several scattered stitches within a short space of each other, use the last stitch as a small quilting stitch carried through to the back of the work. Take the point of the needle into the wadding and travel through the wadding to the area for the next square boss stitch, thereby helping to keep the reverse of the work as neat as possible.

**REVERSE OF WORK**

# Seed stitch

Also known as utility quilting stitch, seed stitch is a fast and versatile filling stitch. It can be worked to any length you prefer.

**TIPS**

- Scatter stitches widely or work them closer together for dense, more compact quilted areas.
- Work stitches in even lengths across your quilt project, or vary them for greater effect and dimension.

**STEP 1**

*Make a quilting stitch through all layers, at any angle and in any direction you like – the distance from the starting point to where the needle enters the fabric will determine the length of the seed stitch.*

**STEP 2**

*Make a second quilting stitch at a different angle to the first. Seed stitches are meant to be placed randomly. If your stitches begin to look uniform, try turning your work.*

**STEP 3**

*If working several scattered stitches within a short space of each other, use the last stitch as a small quilting stitch carried through to the back of the work. Take the point of the needle into the wadding and travel through the wadding to the area for the next stitch. This also means that you will end up with only small seed stitches on the back of the work.*

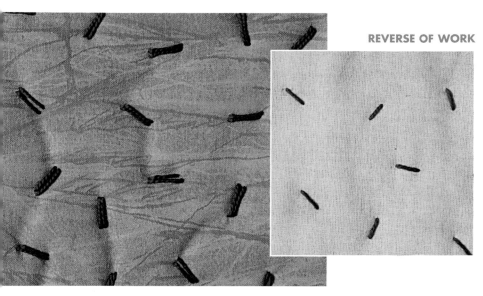

**REVERSE OF WORK**

# Double seed

These double stitches can be worked to any length, and scattered widely or worked close together. For variation, change the length of individual pairs.

**STEP 1**

*Make a quilting stitch through all layers, at any angle and in any direction you like – the distance from the starting point to where the needle enters the fabric will determine the length of the seed stitch.*

**STEP 2**

*Make a second quilting stitch alongside the first one, ensuring that they sit snugly next to each other.*

**STEP 3**

*Make a second set of two stitches, at a different angle to the first pair. Continue in this manner, and try to position the pairs of stitches randomly. Turning your work regularly can help you to head off in another direction.*

**STEP 4**

*If working several scattered double seed stitches within a short space of each other, use the last stitch as a small quilting stitch carried through to the back of the work. Take the point of the needle into the wadding and travel through the wadding to the area for the next pair of stitches. In this way, you will end up with only small seed stitches on the back of the work.*

# Hand-sewn Surface Embellishment

The embellishment techniques and suggestions shown here are additional to your quilted work. They can be valuable decorations to quilt projects such as wallhangings, when further surface interest is required.

Please note that it is inadvisable to add detachable surface embellishments to quilts that will be handled by babies and children.

# *Buttons, charms and beads*

A great variety of buttons, charms and beads are
available, and they can make fun and unusual additions
to quilt work. Dot individual items around or cluster
them together in groups.

## BUTTONS AND CHARMS

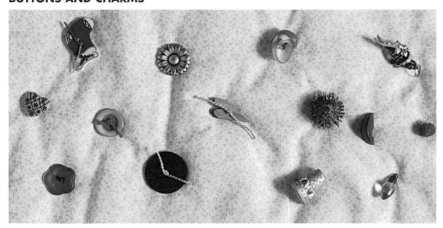

### STEP 1

Bring the thread to the surface
of the work, and take the
needle through the button or
charm. Now either take the
needle back into the fabric
through a second hole in the
item, or loop the thread over the edge of the item and
back into the fabric. Decorative thread can be tied
through the holes and knotted on the surface of the
work for additional texture and interest.

### 🌀 TIPS

• Threads for securing
buttons and charms should
preferably be taken through
all layers of a quilt project
to secure the items tightly.

• Be aware of what is
happening on the back of
the work and, where it is
necessary to have a stitch
appear on the reverse side
of your quilt project, ensure
that it is short and tidy.

### STEP 2

Alternatively, pass the thread through a bead before taking the needle back through the same hole – the bead will secure the thread on top of the button or charm.

### STEP 3

Make a stitch through all layers of the quilt work to secure the item. Finish the stitch with a quilting stitch, or tie and leave the thread as a decorative feature on the surface of your work. Textured or metallic threads are particularly effective used in this way.

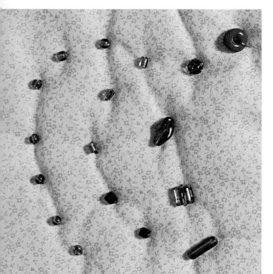

### BEADS
### STEP 1

Choose a needle that will fit through the hole in the bead. Bring the thread to the surface of the work. Pass the needle through the hole in the bead.

### STEP 2

Take the needle back into the fabric close to the spot where the thread initially emerged. Make a short quilting stitch through all layers, forwards, but before pulling the needle through, loop the thread forwards and around the point of the needle. Pull the thread taut before pulling the needle through the fabric. Secure with a quilting stitch. Push the needle through the wadding to the area for the next bead, thereby maintaining a neat appearance on the reverse of the work.

# *Sequins*

Sequins come in all shapes, sizes and colours. They
can provide individual highlights or be clustered
together in groups for massed shimmer and sparkle.

## STEP 1

*Bring the thread to the
surface of the work. Pass
the needle through the
hole in the sequin. Loop
the thread over the edge of
the sequin and take the
needle back into the fabric.*

## STEP 2

*Alternatively, pass the
needle through a bead
before taking it through
the same hole in the
sequin – the bead will
secure the thread on top
of the sequin.*

## STEP 3

*Make a stitch through all
layers of the quilt work to
secure the sequin. Finish
the stitch with a quilting
stitch, or tie and leave the
thread as a decorative
feature on the surface of your work. Textured or
metallic threads are particularly effective used in
this way.*

# Shisha

The word "shisha" means "little mirror". Shisha embroidery is a traditional Indian technique used on clothing and furnishings, in which tiny mirrors are inserted into the design and embroidered to hold them in place. These little mirrors can add a lovely twinkle to your quilt work. Traditionally, shisha are made from cut glass, but you could use a large sequin if you prefer. Do not worry if the edges of the shisha are uneven, because the stitches will cover them.

First of all, a base grid is sewn to hold the mirror in place. The thread needs to be kept taut at all stages during this process. Keep the stitches of the base grid parallel (in both directions), as close to the centre of the mirror as is possible. (Later, when additional embroidery stitches are worked into the base grid, the grid will be pulled outwards a little to uncover the mirror.) If the base grid is too loose or too near the edge of the mirror, it will slip off and fail to keep the mirror in place.

Now additional embroidery stitches can be added for decorative effect. These can be worked very closely together, providing a heavy and dense look. Alternatively, they can be spaced further apart, to make a filigree-like trellis, through which more areas of the mirror will shine.

## CLOSED SHISHA

**STEP 1**

*Hold the mirror in place on the surface of the fabric with your non-sewing thumb (or use fabric glue or double-sided sticky tape if you prefer). Bring the thread to the surface of the work alongside the mirror's edge. Work two horizontal and parallel stitches across the mirror, as close to the centre as you can, making a small stitch on the opposite side of the mirror before returning to the side that you started on.*

*Take the needle into the fabric and bring it out by one of the remaining sides of the mirror. Work two vertical and parallel stitches at right angles to the first pair. Work upwards and away from you, take the needle down behind each of the first stitches in turn and at the edge of the mirror, make a small stitch sideways. This completes the base grid.*

**STEP 2**

*Now take the needle into the fabric and bring it up somewhere alongside the edge of the mirror. Hold the thread forwards and upwards and, working in a clockwise direction, make a blanket stitch down behind the base grid.*

**Closed shisha**

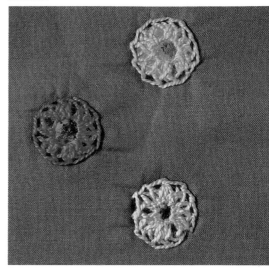

## STEP 3

Hold the thread forwards and downwards and make a chain stitch alongside the edge of the mirror. Repeat steps 3 and 4 until you have worked all the way around the mirror. Secure the last chain by taking the thread into the fabric outside the last chain.

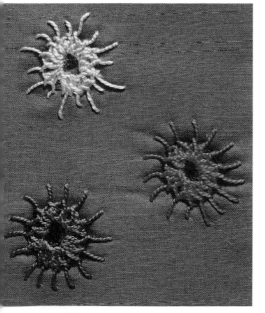

Open shisha

## OPEN SHISHA
### STEP 1

Hold the mirror in position. Bring the thread to the surface alongside the mirror's edge and work a set of double parallel lines across the centre of the mirror. Take the needle into the fabric, come up on one of the remaining sides of the mirror and work a second set of double parallel lines at right angles to the first, weaving the thread over and under the previous set of parallel stitches. This completes the base grid.

Take the needle into the fabric and bring it out somewhere alongside the edge of the mirror. Working in an anticlockwise direction, hold the thread down and around to the right. Make a blanket stitch into the base grid and pull the thread through.

## STEP 2

*Hold the thread down and around to the right. Make a blanket stitch into the fabric, bringing the needle into the waiting loop of thread. As the needle is pulled through, hold the thread across the centre of the mirror and the blanket stitch will sit snugly against the side of the mirror.*

*Continue around the mirror, repeating steps 1 and 2. Secure the last blanket stitch with a quilting stitch outside it.*

> ## TIP
>
> The extra embroidery stitches surrounding the shisha are based on basic chain stitch (see page 77) and basic blanket stitch (see page 104).

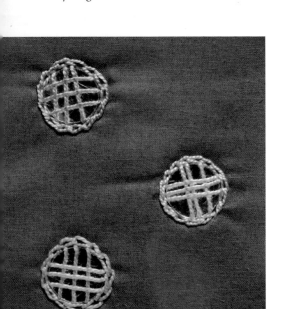

Contemporary shisha

## CONTEMPORARY SHISHA
### STEP 1

*Hold the mirror in position and secure it with a set of three rows of thread, evenly spaced, across the centre of the mirror. Take the needle into the fabric, come up on an unused side of the mirror and stitch a second set of three rows of thread at right angles to the first. This completes the base grid.*

### STEP 2

*Hold the thread forwards and down and, beginning at the top of the mirror and working in an anticlockwise direction, sew a series of chain stitches alongside the edge of the mirror. Secure the final chain stitch with a stitch outside the last link.*

# Couching

The word "couching" is derived from the French word "coucher", which means "to lay something down horizontally". Some threads are too thick, too textured or too weak to be used for the quilting process, which demands that they are constantly passed through layers of fabric and wadding. However, these threads can still be used for embellishment, by placing them on the surface of the work and attaching them to the fabric with a couching stitch. Couching is done using a secondary thread (or several threads) in the same colour as the main thread, or in a strong or subtle contrast. Couched threads can add a great deal of raised texture and decorative interest to the surface of quilt work.

### COUCHED THREAD

Couched threads can be worked in single lines, which are suitable for following quilting designs or for contour-quilting (outlining) motif patterns. You can couch around geometric shapes, curves and circles. The actual thread to be couched can consist of chunky and textured threads, multiple fibres, several strands of thread, fancy ribbons, yarns and so on.

You have two options for starting and finishing the ends of the thread(s) to be couched. If the thread can be accommodated in a needle, it can be brought to the surface of the fabric at the beginning of the line and taken back down through it at the end of the work. You might even find that you can use the traditional quilter's knot to start and

finish. A large-eyed, bodkin-style needle is useful at this stage.

If this approach is not possible, there are other solutions. You can hide the raw edges of the thread under a cluster of securing stitches, or knot the end of the thread and leave it on the surface of the work as a textural feature. Alternatively, you can catch the raw ends of the thread into the seams of the quilt pieces as they are sewn – this needs forward planning into the design and may not be the easiest option.

### COUCHING STITCHES

The stitches used for the actual job of couching – holding down the main thread, which then becomes the couched thread – can be worked singly or in clusters, using straight stitches or diagonal stitches. You can also make use of more decorative, wider stitches. Couching stitches require some space between them to allow the couched thread to remain visible.

You might like to do the job of quilting at the same time as couching. To do this, the couching stitches need to pass through all layers of the quilt work. This is where some of the wider stitches will be useful.

**TIP**

When working long lengths of couched thread, it is advisable to place pins across the thread at regular intervals to hold it in position.

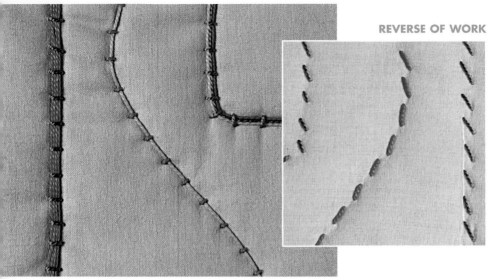

**REVERSE OF WORK**

**SINGLE STITCHES** *Couching with single straight stitches over single thread and multiple threads.*

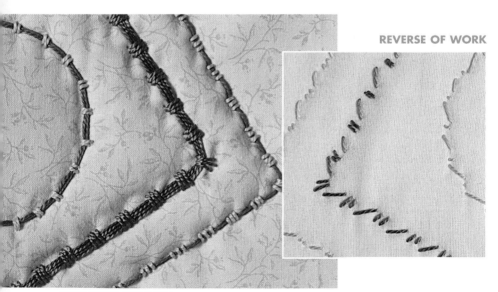

**REVERSE OF WORK**

**CLUSTERED STITCHES** *Couching with clustered straight stitches over single thread and multiple threads.*

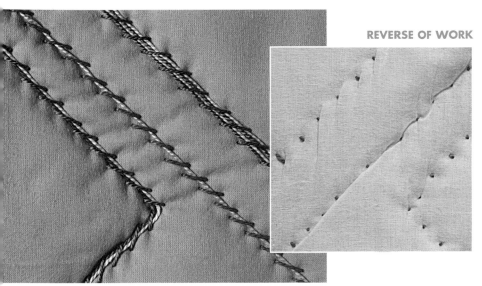

**SINGLE DIAGONAL STITCHES** *Couching with single diagonal stitches over single thread and multiple threads.*

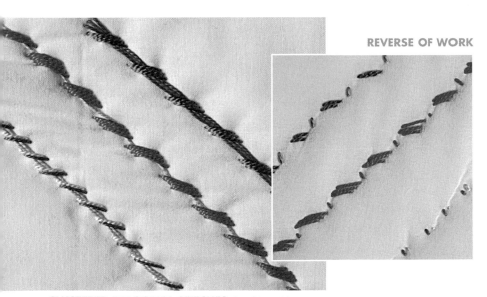

**CLUSTERED DIAGONAL STITCHES** *Couching with clustered diagonal stitches over single thread and multiple threads.*

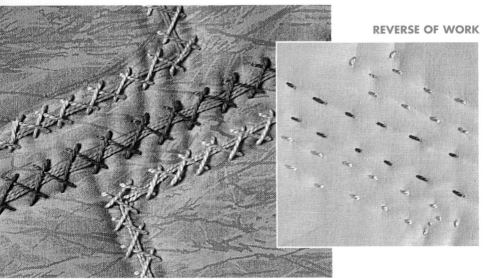

**REVERSE OF WORK**

**HERRINGBONE STITCH** *Couching with basic herringbone stitch (see page 114) over multiple threads.*

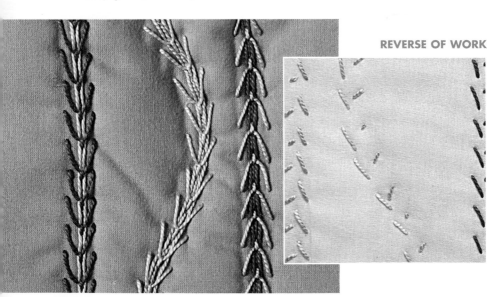

**REVERSE OF WORK**

**FLY STITCH** *Couching with basic fly stitch (see page 99) over multiple threads.*

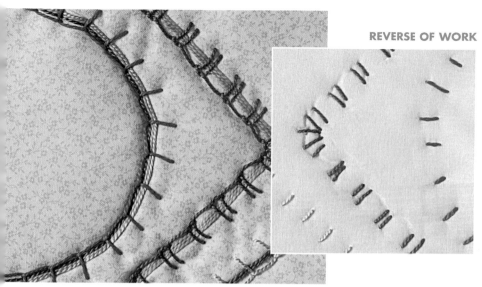

**REVERSE OF WORK**

**BLANKET STITCH** *Couching with single and clustered basic blanket stitch (see page 104) over multiple threads.*

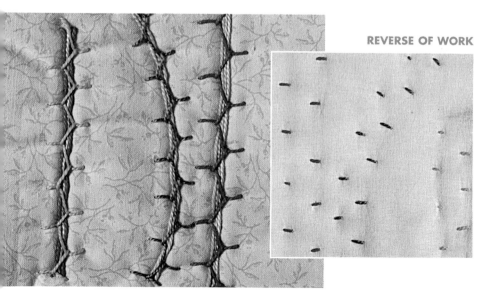

**REVERSE OF WORK**

**CRETAN STITCH** *Couching with basic Cretan stitch (see page 126) over multiple threads.*

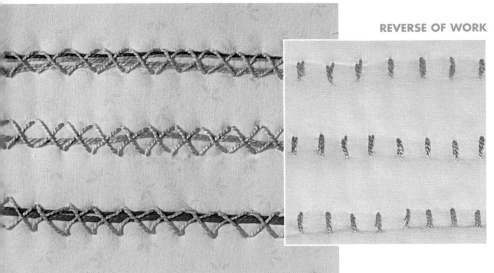

**REVERSE OF WORK**

**CROSS STITCH** *Couching with basic cross stitch (see page 122) over multiple threads.*

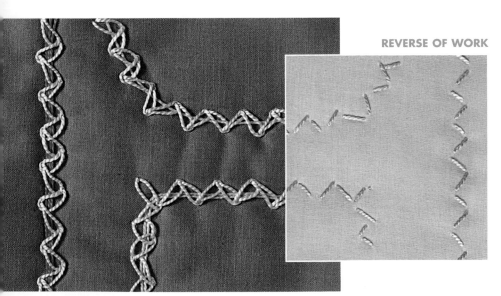

**REVERSE OF WORK**

**ZIGZAG CHAIN** *Couching with basic zigzag chain stitch (see page 91) over single thread and multiple threads.*

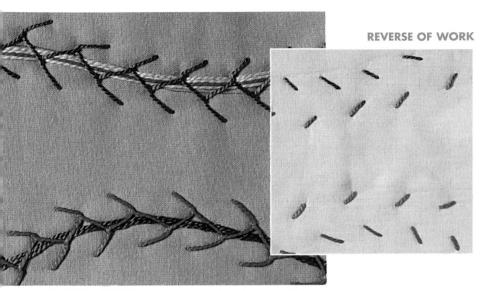

**FEATHER STITCH** *Couching with basic single feather stitch (see page 95) over multiple threads.*

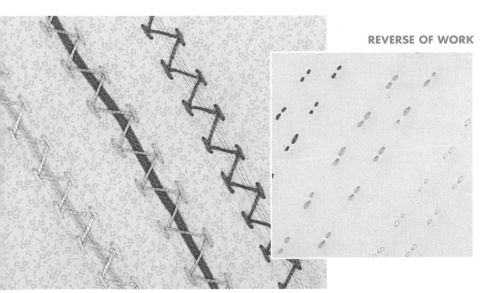

**CHEVRON STITCH** *Couching using basic chevron stitch (see page 132) over multiple threads.*

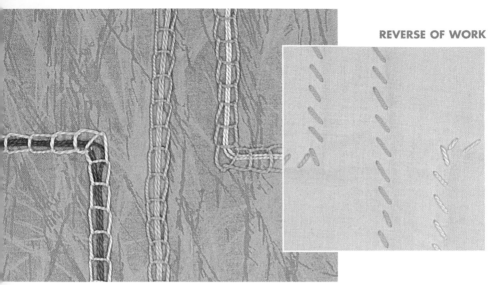

**OPEN CHAIN** *Couching with basic open chain stitch (see page 81) over multiple threads.*

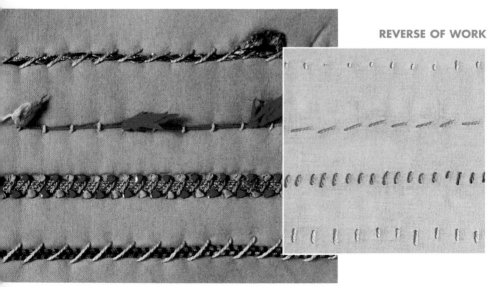

**EMBELLISHMENT** *Couching with single diagonal or straight stitches over fancy threads, yarns, metallics, wool and ribbons.*

# Hand-sewn Insertion Stitches

Insertion stitches provide an interesting alternative method of joining multiple panels to form a quilt. Each individual panel needs a finished edge that is then joined to its neighbouring finished panel with a decorative stitch. Insertion stitches can be worked tightly, so that the panels are next to each other, or worked in a looser fashion, providing a delicate trelliswork of stitching for more decorative projects.

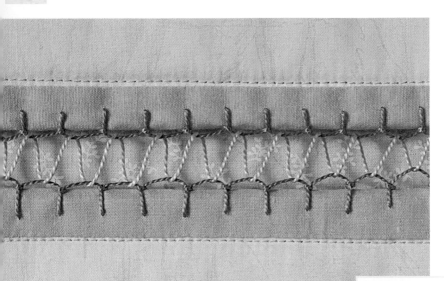

# Laced insertion

This stitch is also known as laced faggot stitch. A looped and knotted stitch is worked along each of the quilt edges, and the lacing is then worked through the loops.

## STEP 1

First, work a row of knotted and looped stitches along each of the quilt edges to be joined. Bring the thread to the surface of the fabric. Hold the thread forwards and wrap the thread around the back of the needle from left to right. Hold this wrapped thread while inserting the needle into the fabric. Before pulling the needle and thread through, wrap the thread around the back of the needle a second time, from right to left. Pull the thread through and a knot will form. Continue along the edge of the fabric. Work a matching set of edging stitches on the second quilt edge.

## STEP 2

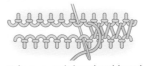

Take a second thread and lace this through the edging stitches, running the needle in and out of the stitches without catching up any fabric as you progress along the line. Secure the lacing thread at the end of the work.

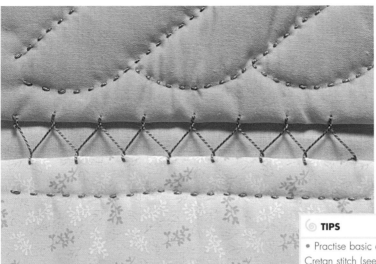

# Open Cretan stitch

Open Cretan stitch makes an easy-to-work and attractive insertion stitch. It is also known as faggoting and herringbone insertion stitch.

**TIPS**

• Practise basic open Cretan stitch (see page 126) first, and you will find it easy to use it for joining two edges of fabric.
• The wrapping of the thread relies on the way the thread is held prior to passing the needle through the fabric.

**STEP 1**

For joining two edges of fabric, bring the thread to the surface at the lower of the two edges. Hold the thread forwards and upwards along the line of work. Make a small, vertical stitch downwards in the upper edge of fabric, bringing the needle into the waiting loop of thread.

**STEP 2**

Hold the thread forwards and downwards along the line of work. Make a small, vertical stitch upwards in the lower edge of fabric, bringing the needle into the waiting loop of thread. Continue in this way along the line of work.

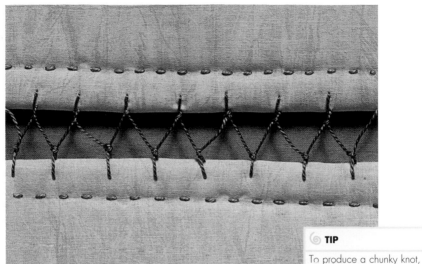

# Knotted insertion

Knotted insertion stitch is also known as knotted faggot stitch. It produces an attractive joining stitch with a pretty knotted finish.

## STEP 1

For joining two edges of fabric, bring the thread to the surface of the fabric at the lower of the two edges. Hold the thread forwards and upwards along the line of work. Make a vertical stitch downwards in the upper edge of fabric and into the waiting loop of thread. Holding the thread forwards once more, take the needle behind the threads of the stitch without catching up any fabric and bring it into the waiting loop of thread for a second time. This will form the knot.

## STEP 2

Hold the thread forwards and downwards along the line of work. Make a vertical stitch upwards in the lower edge of fabric and into the waiting loop of thread. Holding the thread forwards and downwards once more, take the needle behind the threads of the stitch without catching any fabric and bring it into the waiting loop of thread for a second time. Continue in the same way along the line of work.

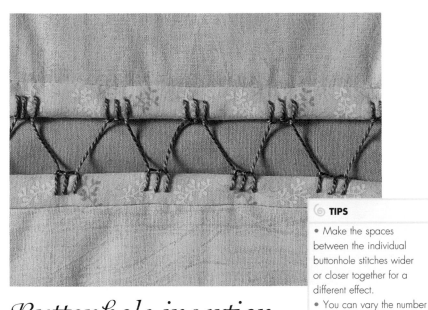

# *Buttonhole insertion*

Buttonhole insertion stitch makes an attractive and strong stitch for joining two quilt edges. Practise basic buttonhole stitch (worked in the same way as blanket stitch, see page 104) first.

see page 104

**TIPS**

• Make the spaces between the individual buttonhole stitches wider or closer together for a different effect.

• You can vary the number of buttonhole stitches from two up to four or five.

**STEP 1**

For joining two edges of fabric, bring the thread to the surface of the fabric at the lower of the two edges. Hold the thread forwards and upwards along the line of work. Make a vertical stitch downwards in the upper edge of fabric, bringing the needle into the waiting loop of thread. Repeat this twice more.

**STEP 2**

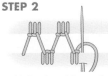

Hold the thread forwards and downwards along the line of work. Make a vertical stitch upwards in the lower edge of fabric, bringing the needle into the waiting loop of thread. Repeat this twice more. Repeat steps 1 and 2 to continue along the line of work.

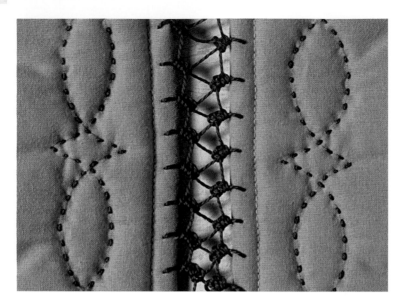

# *Italian insertion*

Italian insertion stitch is also known as Italian buttonhole insertion stitch. When used to join two edges of quilt work together, it provides a decorative latticework of stitches.

**STEP 1**

Working vertically and down towards you, bring the thread to the surface of the fabric on the right-hand quilt edge. Make a small stitch to the fabric on the left-hand quilt edge. Work four buttonhole stitches along the bar of thread between the two edges of fabric, working from left to right.

**STEP 2**

Hold the thread below the work, move further down the line and make a stitch from the right-hand quilt edge, bringing the needle into a loop of thread. Follow this with a stitch from the left-hand quilt edge, further down the work, bringing the needle into a loop of thread.

**STEP 3**

Work four buttonhole stitches over the two threads on the right-hand side of the insertion space, working from centre to right. Make a stitch into a loop of thread on the right-hand quilt edge. Work four buttonhole stitches over the two threads on the left-hand side of the insertion space, working from centre to left. Make a stitch into a loop of thread on the left-hand quilt edge and repeat steps 2 and 3 to continue along the line of work.

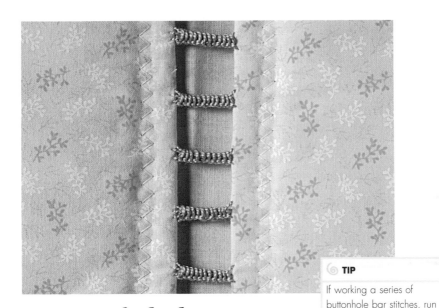

# Buttonhole bar

A strong, individual linking stitch suitable for joining two quilt edges. Each bar is constructed from two lengths of thread, covered with basic buttonhole stitch (worked in the same way as blanket stitch, see page 104).

> **TIP**
>
> If working a series of buttonhole bar stitches, run the thread between the bars through the wadding and/or fabrics of the two quilt edges for added strength.

**STEP 1**

Bring the thread to the surface of the fabric on the left-hand quilt edge. Form a bar between the two edges. Make a small stitch from the right-hand quilt edge, followed by a second stitch from the left-hand quilt edge (make between two and five stitches, depending on how heavy you would like the bar to appear).

**STEP 2**

Cover each set of long base stitches with a row of tightly worked basic buttonhole stitch (sewn in the same way as blanket stitch, see page 104). If working several bars in a row, run the thread through the fabric and/or wadding of the quilt edges in order to move to the next area to be worked.

# Stitches for Machine Quilting

It is possible to machine quilt a project with a simple running stitch or zigzag stitch, however many modern sewing machines come with a selection of decorative stitches that can all be used for quilting.

It's important to check what is happening on the reverse of your quilt, whether you are quilting by hand or by machine. A row of machined stitches is heavier, stiffer and more densely worked than hand-sewn stitches.

# *Straight stitch*

Straight stitch is the most versatile of all the stitches that a sewing machine will do. The stitch length can be elongated or reduced to suit the required end appearance. It is just as easy to sew a straight line as it is to sew a curved line or a corner.

**STRAIGHT LINE**

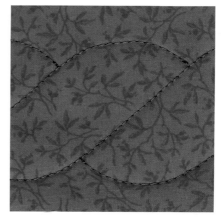

**CURVED LINE**

**REVERSE OF WORK**

**GEOMETRIC/CORNER**

# *Zigzag stitch*

The width and length of zigzag stitch can be adjusted to vary its appearance. For a gently tapering result, reduce the width of the stitch as it is being sewn. Keep the needle in the fabric and pivot the work to turn corners.

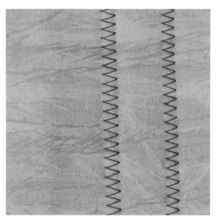

**STRAIGHT LINE**

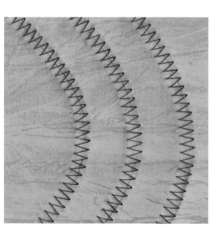

**CURVED LINE**

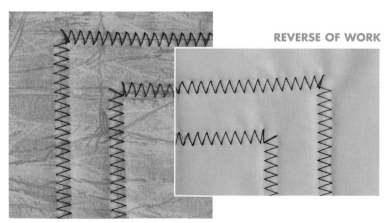

**GEOMETRIC/CORNER**

**REVERSE OF WORK**

## USE THIS STITCH FOR

- straight lines
- curved lines
- geometric designs
- corners
- decorative alternative to zigzag

# *Elastic blind hem*

This stitch is generally provided for hemming stretchy fabrics, but it offers a decorative alternative to ordinary zigzag stitch when worked on woven fabrics and quilt projects. Reducing the length of the stitch will bring the peaks of the stitch closer together.

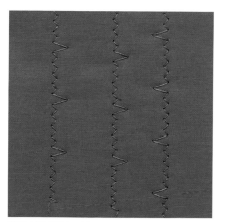

**STRAIGHT LINE**

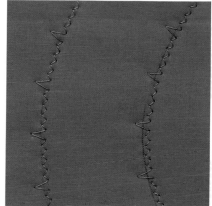

**CURVED LINE**

**REVERSE OF WORK**

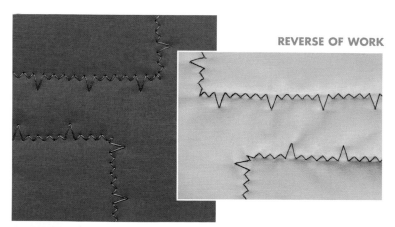

**GEOMETRIC/CORNER**

# *Elastic stitch*

Elastic stitch is primarily provided for sewing elastic to garments – the stitch will stretch with the elastic when it is pulled. This stitch provides an alternative to ordinary zigzag stitch and can be used when a firmer zigzag stitch is required.

### ﹨﹨ USE THIS STITCH FOR

- straight lines
- curved lines
- geometric designs
- corners
- a firmer alternative to zigzag stitch

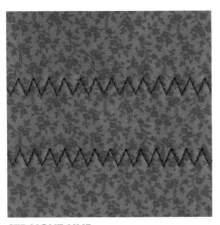

**STRAIGHT LINE**

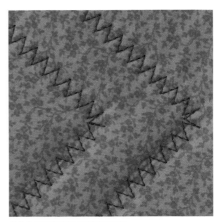

**GEOMETRIC/CORNER**

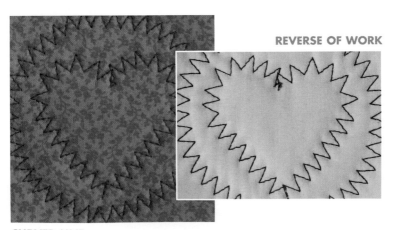

**CURVED LINE**

**REVERSE OF WORK**

# Closed overlock stitch

Closed overlock stitch is another stitch that is primarily provided as a stretch stitch for elastic or jersey fabrics. It makes a useful quilting stitch and gives a dense and busy finish to the quilting line.

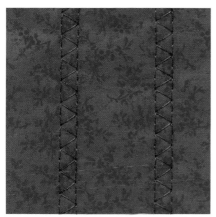

**STRAIGHT LINE**

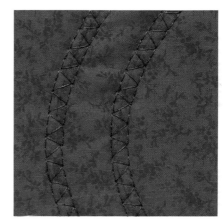

**CURVED LINE**

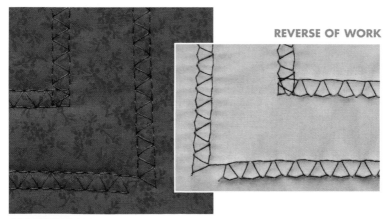

**REVERSE OF WORK**

**GEOMETRIC/CORNER**

# *Buttonhole stitch*

Machine-sewn buttonhole stitch closely resembles hand-sewn blanket stitch (see page 104). It is as easy to sew this stitch on a curve or corner as it is to sew it on a straight line, although care must be taken when pivoting the work around the needle on a sharp corner.

(see page 104)

## ⫶⫶⫶ USE THIS STITCH FOR

- straight lines
- curved lines
- geometric designs
- corners

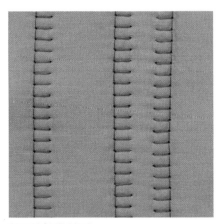

**STRAIGHT LINE**

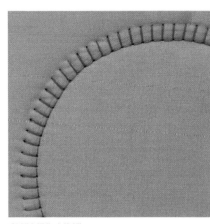

**CURVED LINE**

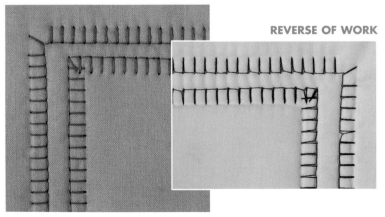

**GEOMETRIC/CORNER**

**REVERSE OF WORK**

## ⸙ USE THIS STITCH FOR

- straight lines
- curved lines
- geometric designs
- corners
- decorative
  feathered effect

# *Bridging stitch*

Bridging stitch is primarily provided on a sewing machine for joining two pieces of fabric together with a decorative stitch rather than a seam. Used as a quilting stitch, it has a similar finished appearance to the hand-sewn single feather stitch (see page 95).

**STRAIGHT LINE**

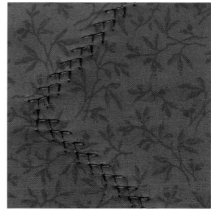

**GEOMETRIC/CORNER**

**REVERSE OF WORK**

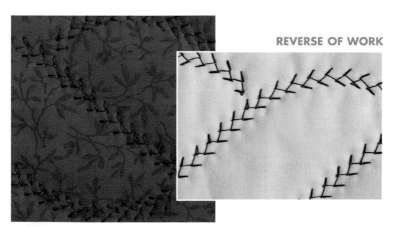

**CURVED LINE**

# Pullover stitch

This standard utility stitch is offered for joining open-knit and heavy knit fabrics, but it also creates a very attractive quilting stitch. It is easy to sew on curves and corners, as well as on straight lines.

**STRAIGHT LINE**

**GEOMETRIC/CORNER**

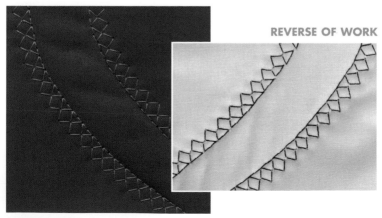

**REVERSE OF WORK**

**CURVED LINE**

## USE THIS STITCH FOR

- straight lines
- curved lines
- geometric designs
- corners
- adding movement to a design

# Open overlock stitch

Another utility stitch, primarily offered for joining fabric edges or overlocking the edges of fabrics that do not fray excessively. For quilters, it provides a diagonal variation on buttonhole/blanket stitch which, in itself, adds movement to a quilting design.

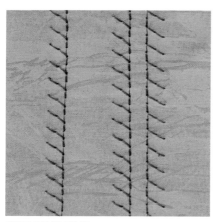

**STRAIGHT LINE**

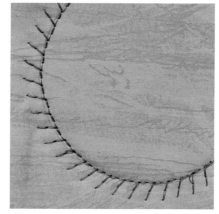

**CURVED LINE**

**REVERSE OF WORK**

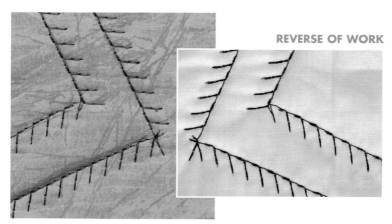

**GEOMETRIC/CORNER**

# Waves stitch (preset)

Some of the more curvilinear stitches found in the preset selection on sewing machines can add a lot of extra movement to a quilting design, whether used on a straight line, curved line or geometric line. This pattern of waves is fun to use for quilting.

**STRAIGHT LINE**

**CURVED LINE**

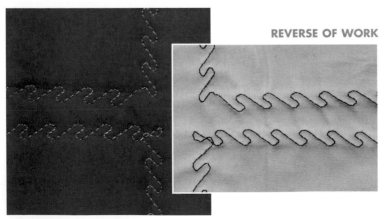

**GEOMETRIC/CORNER**

**REVERSE OF WORK**

## ◊◊ USE THIS STITCH FOR

- straight lines
- curved lines
- geometric designs
- corners
- textural interest
- eye-catching
  repeated motif

# *Stars stitch (preset)*

Motif stitches such as these stars can be found among the preset stitch selection on a sewing machine. When used as a quilting stitch, they can add extra textural interest as well as visual appeal to your quilt work.

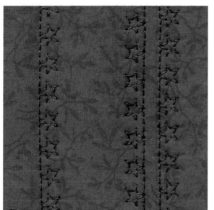

**STRAIGHT LINE**

**CURVED LINE**

**REVERSE OF WORK**

**GEOMETRIC/CORNER**

# Hearts stitch (preset)

Some of the wider stitches in the preset selection of machine stitches, such as this heart, make decorative quilting stitches. If a stitch is "one-sided", as the heart motif is, you need to consider which side of the quilting line you would like the motif to sit on.

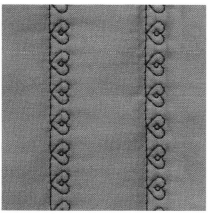

**STRAIGHT LINE**

**CURVED LINE**

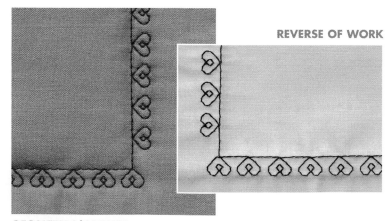

**REVERSE OF WORK**

**GEOMETRIC/CORNER**

- straight lines
- curved lines
- geometric designs
- corners
- simple quilting designs

# Geometric stitch (preset)

Some preset stitches are wide and dense in appearance, as demonstrated by the geometric "Roman key" stitch shown here. These wide and heavier stitches are better used for more open and basic quilt designs, rather than smaller, intricate patterns.

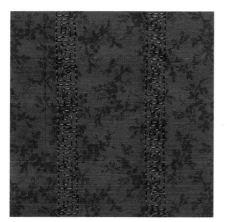

**STRAIGHT LINE**

**CURVED LINE**

**REVERSE OF WORK**

**GEOMETRIC/CORNER**

# Twin-needle zigzag

Using the twin-needle facility on your sewing machine can add fun and colour to a quilting project. It adds extra definition to the chosen stitches. Use the same colour thread in each needle, or two contrasting threads for greater effect.

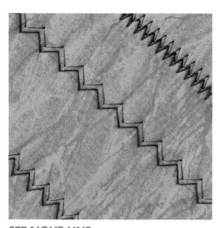

**STRAIGHT LINE**

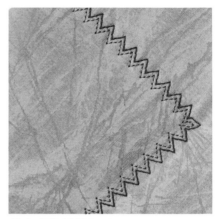

**GEOMETRIC/CORNER**

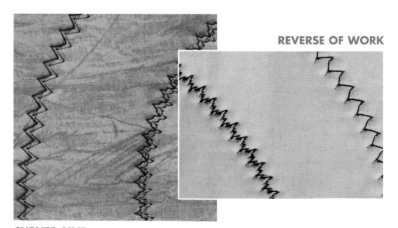

**CURVED LINE**

**REVERSE OF WORK**

### ⚒ USE THIS STITCH FOR

- straight lines
- curved lines
- geometric designs
- corners

# *Twin-needle decorative stitches*

The twin-needle facility on a sewing machine does not have to be used purely for simple stitches; it can also be used to great effect for a selection of preset stitches. Using two different coloured threads will provide a "shadow" effect to the line of quilting.

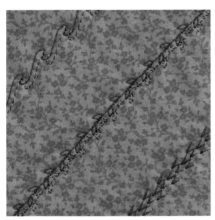

**STRAIGHT LINE**

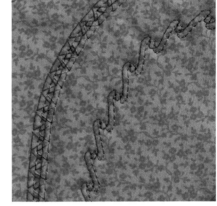

**CURVED LINE**

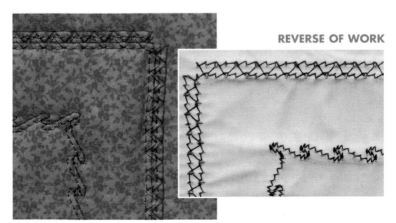

**GEOMETRIC/CORNER**

**REVERSE OF WORK**

# Machine-sewn Surface Embellishment

Embellishments can be added to your project at different stages during quilt construction. If the quilt top is a single layer, the added embellishment will appear only on the surface of the work. If the quilt layers have already been put together, the machined stitches will pass through all layers and also be seen on the back of the work – an important consideration in some projects.

If further embellishment is needed at the quilting stage of a project, decorative thread and fabric scraps can be anchored by machine quilting.

## ❀ MATERIALS

- cord
- braid
- yarn
- metallic thread

# *Couching*

Add extra textural interest to quilt work by "couching" a ribbon or thread – lay it on top of the quilt and couch it in place with a decorative stitch such as zigzag, elastic stitch, overlocking stitch or any of the wider, preset decorative stitches.

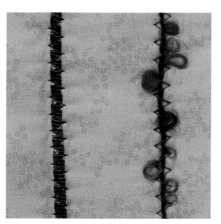

**STRAIGHT LINE**

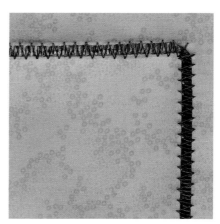

**GEOMETRIC/CORNER**

**CURVED LINE**

**REVERSE OF WORK**

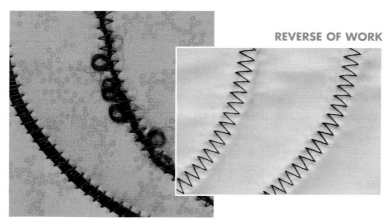

# Fabric manipulation

Use fabric manipulation to add extra textural interest. Try slashing – layer different coloured fabrics, sew together in channels, then cut the top fabrics between the channels to reveal the layered colours. The raw edges of fabric provide surface interest.

 **TIP**

Small sharp scissors or a specialist slashing tool can be used for cutting through fabric layers. A soft brush or the use of a washing machine can also add extra texture to slashed areas.

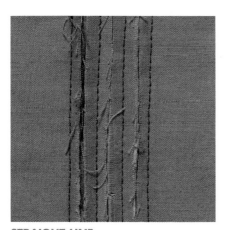

**STRAIGHT LINE**

**CURVED LINE**

**REVERSE OF WORK**

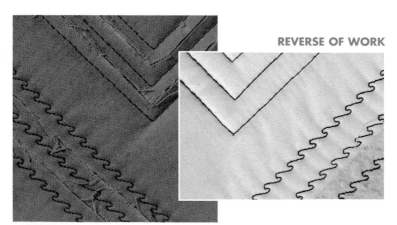

**GEOMETRIC/CORNER AND STRAIGHT LINE WITH PRESET WAVE STITCH**

> ## 6 TIP
> Turned-edge appliqué does not need additional stitching to reinforce the edges. Use reinforcing stitches for raw-edge appliqué and/or fabric that has been bonded into place.

# Machine-sewn appliqué

Motifs can be appliquéd to a quilt: stitch them during construction, or at the quilting stage (when the stitches can be taken through all layers to do the job of quilting in addition to actually reinforcing the appliqué shapes). Use a straight stitch or a decorative stitch.

**ZIGZAG STITCH**

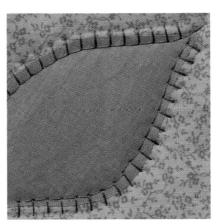

**BLANKET STITCH**

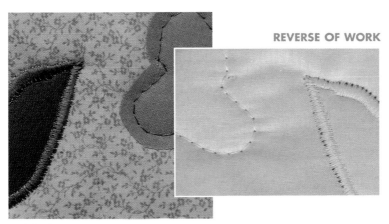

**SATIN STITCH AND STRAIGHT STITCH**

**REVERSE OF WORK**

# Machine-sewn Insertion and Construction Stitches

Any of the more decorative and wider stitches to be found on modern sewing machines can be used for joining together multiple panels to make a quilt. Each individual panel will need a finished edge before it can be joined to its neighbouring panel. The panels need to be close together as sewing machine stitches are limited in how wide they can be worked – the maximum width is generally 1 cm (³⁄₈ in.).

**ENLARGED VIEW**

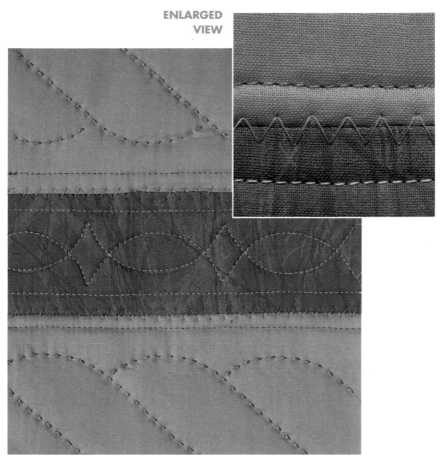

# *Zigzag stitch*

Zigzag stitch and its variations can all be used to join blocks of patchwork that have a finished edge. Construction stitches need to be wide enough to secure the two edges firmly – you will probably need to set the stitch width to its widest setting. The two edges to be joined need to butt up close together without overlapping.

### ⫶ USE THIS STITCH FOR

Joining neatened edges of quilt blocks where no gap is required between edges.

**ENLARGED VIEW**

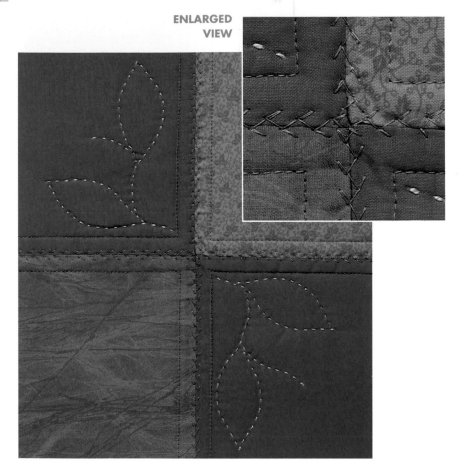

# *Bridging stitch*

Many sewing machines come with a selection of
stitches known as bridging stitches – these are
specifically designed for joining two pieces of fabric
together. Set the stitch width to its widest setting; the
stitch length can be reduced or elongated for a different
effect. The two finished edges of the quilt blocks need
to butt up against each other.

### ⦚ USE THIS STITCH FOR

• Joining multiple quilt
blocks with neatened
edges.
• When a more decorative
effect is required.
• Where a stronger stitch
is required.

**ENLARGED
VIEW**

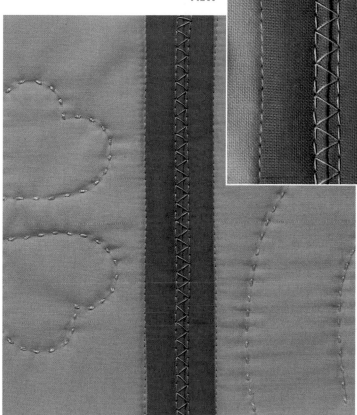

# Closed overlock stitch

Most sewing machines offer some sort of overlocking
stitch – these stitches are wide enough to be used for
joining two finished quilt edges together. Set the stitch
width to its widest setting; the stitch length can be
altered to suit the required finished effect. The edges of
the fabric must butt up against each other.

## ✂ USE THIS STITCH FOR

- Joining quilt blocks with finished edges.
- When a stronger stitch is required.

# Quilting Your Patchwork

Your chosen quilting design should enhance the patchwork in your quilt project, but not overwhelm it. Choose a quilting pattern that reflects the design of your entire quilt.

Interesting contrasts can be provided by working geometric patterns on curves and vice versa, adding movement and visual interest to what might be an otherwise unexciting quilt. Quilt "in the ditch" with a traditional quilting stitch if you don't want the quilting to detract from the design of the patchwork.

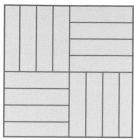

**PATCHWORK BLOCK**

# *Rail fence*

Rail fence is based on strips of patchwork. Long strips of fabric are joined together; the resulting fabric "scarf" is then cut across to make units for piecing together to form various patterns. The simplicity of the patchwork pattern allows scope for a variety of quilting designs.

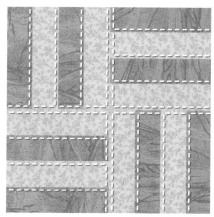

**CONTOUR-QUILTING**

**GEOMETRIC DESIGN**

**CURVILINEAR DESIGN: SPIRAL**

 **TIP**

A simple quilting design is all that is required to highlight the simplicity of this strip-patchwork technique.

# Log cabin

Log cabin patchwork is one of the oldest patterns and has been used extensively, both historically and geographically. This block is constructed using strips of fabric and working in a circular direction emanating outwards from the central square.

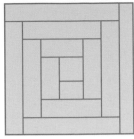

**PATCHWORK BLOCK**

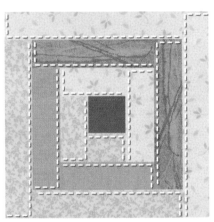

**CONTOUR-QUILTING**

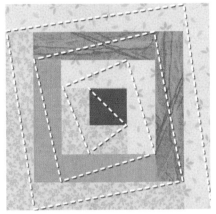

**GEOMETRIC DESIGN: STRAIGHT LINE SPIRAL**

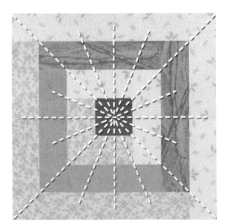

**GEOMETRIC DESIGN: STARBURST**

 **TIP**

The quilting designs and stitches chosen will depend on the width of the "logs" sewn and the number of seams present to be quilted through.

**PATCHWORK BLOCK**

# Crazy patchwork

Crazy patchwork was a favourite of nineteenth-century quilters. Quilts using this design would often incorporate heavy, textured fabrics, such as velvets and brocades, and the use of surface embellishment. Crazy patchwork can be hand-sewn or machine-sewn.

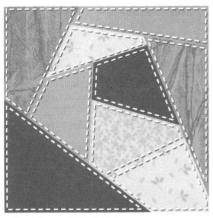

**CONTOUR-QUILTING**

 **TIP**

Crazy patchwork involves a lot of seams and bulky areas – both factors that will determine the method of quilting, quilting design and the stitches that you choose to use.

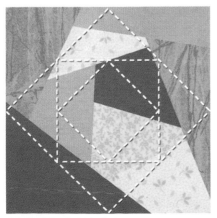

**GEOMETRIC DESIGN:
SQUARE WITHIN A SQUARE**

**CURVILINEAR DESIGN:
FREEHAND CURVES**

# Pinwheel (2 x 2 grid)

"Pinwheel" is a patchwork block designed on a 2 x 2 grid (four squares in total). With careful fabric placement, an optical illusion of movement can be achieved, making it look like a rotating windmill. Quilting designs can be simple, such as quilting in the ditch, or contour-quilting around the individual patches.

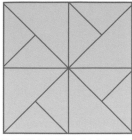

**PATCHWORK BLOCK**

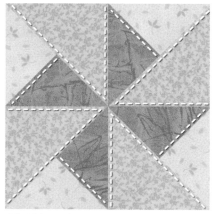

**CONTOUR-QUILTING**

 **TIP**

The "movement" can be highlighted further by the use of circles or spirals. This simple patchwork block provides an ideal canvas for trying out different types of quilting and different stitches.

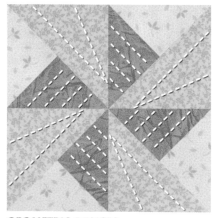

**GEOMETRIC DESIGN: ECHOING MOVEMENT**

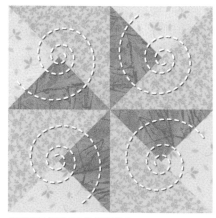

**CURVILINEAR DESIGN: QUARTERED SPIRALS**

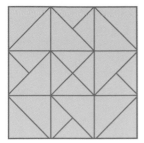

**PATCHWORK BLOCK**

# Card trick (3 x 3 grid)

This ever-popular patchwork pattern uses an optical illusion to place four "playing cards" within a square. Careful fabric placement ensures that the cards seem to overlap one another.

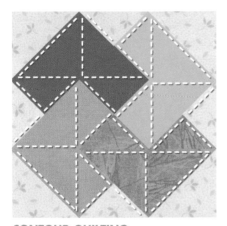

**CONTOUR-QUILTING**

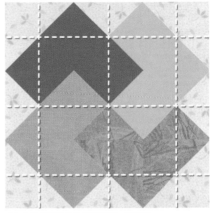

**GEOMETRIC DESIGN: GRID**

**CURVILINEAR DESIGN: HEARTS STENCIL**

**⑥ TIP**

There are a lot of seams used to construct this block, and this will determine which method of quilting and which stitches you choose.

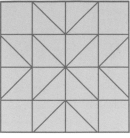

# *Star (4 x 4 grid)*

There is an endless variety of patchwork blocks offering "star" patterns. This interesting variation is based on a geometric 4 x 4 grid (sixteen squares in total). More emphasis can be placed on the star by quilting in the ditch or contour-quilting around the individual patches that represent the star itself.

**PATCHWORK BLOCK**

**CONTOUR-QUILTING**

**GEOMETRIC DESIGN**

 **TIP**

As an alternative, place a quilt stencil design over the entire block to add further visual interest.

**CURVILINEAR DESIGN: FLEUR-DE-LYS STENCIL**

# Mariner's compass (no grid)

Many patchwork blocks, such as this one, are not designed on a formal grid. The "compass" can be kept fairly simple, or added to with extra "spikes" at additional "compass settings", along with intricate piecing of the central circle. A simple quilting design is all that is necessary for this patchwork block.

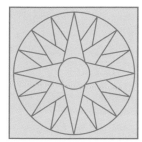

**PATCHWORK BLOCK**

 **TIP**

Use busy quilting stitches in moderation so they do not detract from the pattern itself.

**CONTOUR-QUILTING**

**GEOMETRIC DESIGN: STARBURST**

**CURVILINEAR DESIGN: CIRCLES**

# Drunkard's path (curved-seam patchwork)

Sewing curved-seam patchwork is just as easy to do by hand as by machine. The seam allowance will naturally fall to one side of the curve and this may dictate how and where you quilt this block. A quilting design that uses curves will accentuate the visual "movement" provided by the curved-seam patchwork.

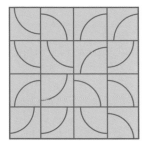

**PATCHWORK BLOCK**

 **TIP**

There is plenty of scope for quilting with different stitches within this block, which will add further textural interest.

**CONTOUR-QUILTING**

**GEOMETRIC DESIGN:
DIRECTIONAL**

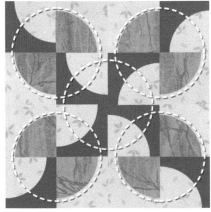

**CURVILINEAR DESIGN:
OVERLAPPING CIRCLES**

# Dutchman's puzzle (triangles)

Many patchwork patterns, such as this one, are constructed using triangles only. In this block, "geese" are clearly seen flying outwards from the centre of the block, in four different directions. The emphasis of the pattern can change according to fabric placement.

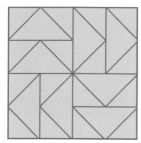

**PATCHWORK BLOCK**

 **TIP**

Place a curved quilting design over the complete block to add an interesting contrast to the geometric patchwork piecing.

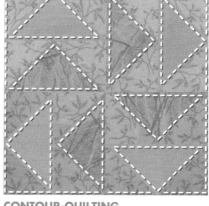

**CONTOUR-QUILTING**

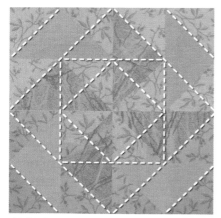

**GEOMETRIC DESIGN:
SQUARE WITHIN A SQUARE**

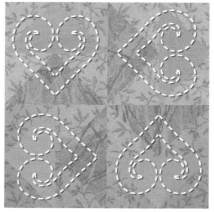

**CURVILINEAR DESIGN:
HEARTS STENCIL**

# Trip around the world (squares)

Many patchwork quilts are constructed entirely from squares of fabric. This idea can also be interpreted within one patchwork block, as shown here. The geometric pattern lends itself well to a variety of straight-line quilting designs.

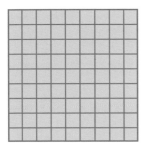

**PATCHWORK BLOCK**

 **TIP**

The high number of closely spaced seam allowances and small squares of different fabrics will require the use of simple quilting stitches.

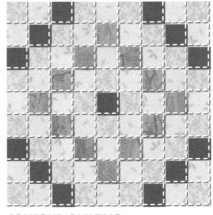

**CONTOUR-QUILTING**

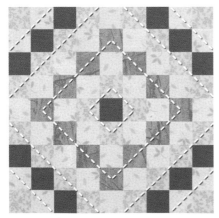

**GEOMETRIC DESIGN: FOLLOWING COLOURWAY**

**GEOMETRIC DESIGN: DIRECTIONAL**

# Tumbling blocks (hexagons and diamonds)

This is just one of numerous patchwork patterns that are constructed using either hexagons or diamonds, or a combination of both. The optical illusion of cubes placed on top of each other is achieved by careful fabric placement, making use of tonal values in the fabrics. Use a curved quilting design to add visual "movement".

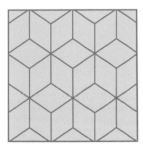

**PATCHWORK BLOCK**

 **TIP**

This design is generally quilted in the ditch, or the individual patches are contour-quilted to emphasize the pattern.

**CONTOUR-QUILTING**

**GEOMETRIC DESIGN: HIGHLIGHTING THE PATTERN**

**CURVILINEAR DESIGN: WAVES/CURVES**

# Flying geese (three-dimensional patchwork)

Three-dimensional patchwork is achieved by fabric manipulation. The "geese" triangles are raised and sit above the surrounding pieced fabrics. Care needs to be taken when quilting three-dimensional patchwork. The raised fabric is often on the bias and, therefore, easy to stretch out of shape.

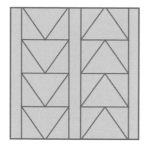

**PATCHWORK BLOCK**

 **TIP**

Ensure that any chosen quilting design will fit within the areas surrounding (or behind) the raised fabrics.

**CONTOUR-QUILTING**

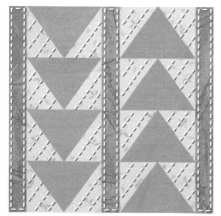

**GEOMETRIC DESIGN: DIRECTIONAL**

**CURVILINEAR DESIGN: STIPPLE (FREE-FORM)**

# *Secret garden (folded patchwork)*

Folded patchwork patterns rely on fabric manipulation. The raised areas of folded fabric add extra textural interest to the patchwork block and will determine how and where the block is quilted. Contour-quilt around the raised fabric areas to add emphasis to them.

**PATCHWORK BLOCK**

 **TIP**

Quilting across the "background" fabric and over the areas where the squares are joined together will strengthen the seams.

**CONTOUR-QUILTING**

**GEOMETRIC DESIGN: DIAGONAL LINES**

**CURVILINEAR DESIGN: STIPPLE (FREE-FORM)**

# Wholecloth border

A simple border of plain fabric can be added to any quilt, whether it has a busy, pieced patchwork centre, or not. Further interest can be added to a plain fabric border by the use of a variety of quilting designs and stitches.

**BORDER PATTERN**

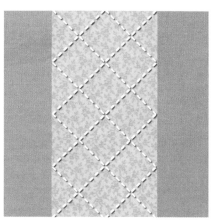

**GEOMETRIC DESIGN:
CROSS-HATCHING**

**CURVILINEAR DESIGN:
HEARTS STENCIL**

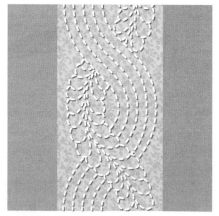

**CURVILINEAR DESIGN:
FEATHER AND CABLE STENCIL**

 **TIP**

The lack of patchwork seams within the plain fabric border provides a wonderful canvas for endless creativity and the use of experimental quilting.

# Pieced chequerboard border

If further interest is required at the outer edge of a quilt, or the quilt needs to be made bigger, one or two (or more) patchwork-pieced borders can be added. These can be made from simple squares, or can be more complex. The design should highlight the pieced border pattern, thereby carrying the design of the quilt outwards to its edges.

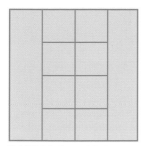

**BORDER PATTERN**

 **TIP**

Choose a quilting design that accentuates the patchwork piecing.

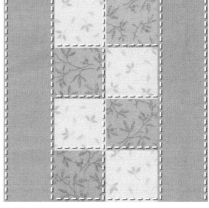

**CONTOUR-QUILTING**

**GEOMETRIC DESIGN**

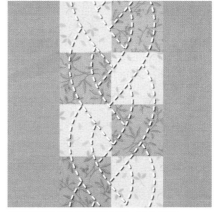

**CURVILINEAR DESIGN: PLAITED DESIGN STENCIL**

# Quilting Your Appliqué

Appliquéd motifs can be further enhanced by quilting around the motif outline. This will add dimension to the quilt.

If the appliqué shapes are quite small, outline quilting will be sufficient. If the shapes are on the large side, they may require quilting inside the shapes themselves. The method of appliqué used and any resulting bulky areas of fabric will determine if you use hand or machine quilting.

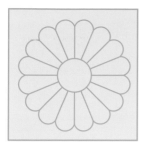

**APPLIQUÉ BLOCK**

# Dresden plate

The Dresden plate pattern is one of the most popular and recognizable appliqué patterns in quilt-making. The number of "petals" can range from as few as twelve up to as many as twenty. Contour-quilt each individual petal to emphasize the pattern.

**CONTOUR-QUILTING**

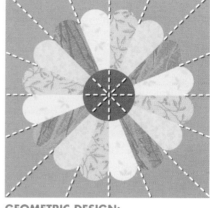

**GEOMETRIC DESIGN: RADIATING LINES**

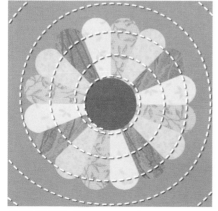

**CURVILINEAR DESIGN: SPIRAL**

 **TIP**

A design that is taken outside the ring of "petals" can effectively quilt the background fabric at the same time.

# Wreath

There are numerous "wreath" patterns to be found among appliqué designs. Variations can be made in the number and style of flowers and leaves, and whether or not a circular "vine" is included. The style of the wreath can be highlighted effectively by contour-quilting the flowers, leaves etc.

**APPLIQUÉ BLOCK**

 **TIP**

Use an infill pattern to quilt the background fabric and add emphasis to the appliqué.

**CONTOUR-QUILTING**

**GEOMETRIC DESIGN: DIAGONAL INFILL LINES**

**CURVILINEAR DESIGN: ECHO QUILTING**

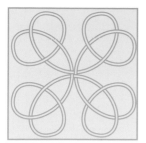

**APPLIQUÉ BLOCK**

# Celtic knot (bias strip)

A Celtic knot design is based on overlapping curves and circles, and the appliquéd knot is formed by a series of "under and over" junctions using bias-cut fabric strips. Celtic knots can be simple or very elaborate. Choose a quilting design that accentuates the flowing lines of the pattern.

**CONTOUR-QUILTING**

**GEOMETRIC DESIGN: DIAGONAL INFILL LINES**

**CURVILINEAR DESIGN: STIPPLE (FREE-FORM)**

 **TIP**

Bias strip appliqué can be used for curved designs where a prominent line is needed. Use the areas of background fabric for interesting quilting designs and/or stitches.

# Tulip (stained glass appliqué)

Highlight the use of bias-cut fabric strips by adding patches of extra "background" fabric within the spaces of the pattern, thereby giving the illusion of stained glass. This form of appliqué lends itself to contour-quilting and echo quilting, which emphasize the raised edges of the fabric strips and make the stained glass effect more realistic.

**APPLIQUÉ BLOCK**

 **TIP**

Use interesting stitches to quilt the surrounding background fabric.

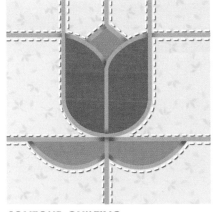

**CONTOUR-QUILTING**

**GEOMETRIC DESIGN:
CROSS-HATCHED INFILL**

**CURVILINEAR DESIGN:
ECHO QUILTING**

**APPLIQUÉ BLOCK**

# Hawaiian appliqué

Patterns for Hawaiian appliqué are numerous and individual to the maker. They are achieved by folding paper and cutting out designs (similar to the snowflake cutouts that children love to make in winter), which are then interpreted in fabric.

**CONTOUR-QUILTING**

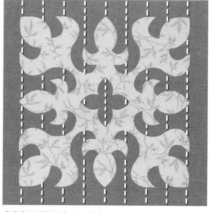

**GEOMETRIC DESIGN: INFILL LINES**

**CURVILINEAR DESIGN: ECHO QUILTING**

 **TIP**

Intricate patterns require simple contour-quilting or echo quilting, which does not detract from the elaborate design of the appliqué.

# Broderie Perse appliqué

Broderie Perse appliqué is achieved by cutting large motifs from printed fabric and placing them on a contrasting background fabric. It usually takes the form of a display of flowers within a basket or vase. The raw edges of the motifs are secured with a variety of decorative embroidery stitches.

**APPLIQUÉ BLOCK**

**TIP**

Simple quilting designs will help to emphasize the appliqué. Knotting and tufting can add extra textural interest to the background areas.

**CONTOUR-QUILTING**

**GEOMETRIC DESIGN: INFILL LINES, CONTRASTING DIRECTIONS**

**CURVILINEAR DESIGN: ECHO QUILTING WITH KNOTTING AND TUFTING**

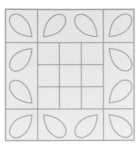

**APPLIQUÉ BLOCK**

# *Appliqué on pieced patchwork block*

Mixing appliquéd shapes with a pieced patchwork block can add dimension and interest to simple patchwork. Contour-quilting or echo quilting around the areas of additional appliqué will add definition.

**CONTOUR-QUILTING**

**TIP**

If an overall design is preferred, sew simple quilting designs over the seams of both the patchwork and the appliqué. Use simple quilting stitches that won't detract from the patchwork/appliqué pattern.

**GEOMETRIC DESIGN: "TRIP AROUND THE WORLD" DESIGN**

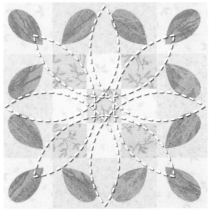

**CURVILINEAR DESIGN: DAISY STENCIL**

# Quilt Edge Finishings

There are several ways to complete the final edge of your quilt, and it's worth giving this some time and thought.

Adding the right binding fabric can soften the effect of an overvibrant quilt or, in turn, give the required visual lift to a mediocre or subdued quilt.

If a binding fabric is too intrusive for your quilt design, the quilt edges can be turned inwards and the quilt finished with no additional binding.

Whichever way you choose to finish your quilt, try to ensure that the finishing edge is sympathetic to the overall design of the quilt.

# Binding using backing fabric

The backing fabric on a quilt can be folded forwards and used to provide an attractive binding that is already part of the quilt. Bear this in mind when selecting backing fabric.

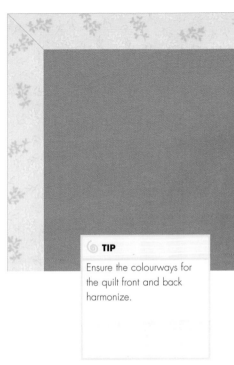

## STEP 1

*When the quilting is finished, trim the wadding back to the same size as the quilt top. Leave the backing fabric at least 2.5 cm (1 in.) wider than the quilt top and wadding on all edges of the quilt.*

**TIP**

Ensure the colourways for the quilt front and back harmonize.

## STEP 2

*At each corner of the quilt, make one fold in the backing fabric so the point of the fold touches the corner of the quilt top. Make a second fold equal to the first.*

## STEP 3

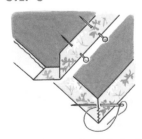

*Fold in the raw edge of the binding on one edge of the quilt; fold in the binding towards the quilt top and pin in place. Repeat with the second side of the binding, so the two edges of binding meet diagonally at the corner of the quilt. Pin and stitch in place. Repeat on all corners of the quilt.*

# Folded-in edges

Achieve a neat, unobtrusive finish by folding the raw edges of the backing and quilt top fabrics inwards. Secure the raw edges with a quilting stitch just inside the folded edge.

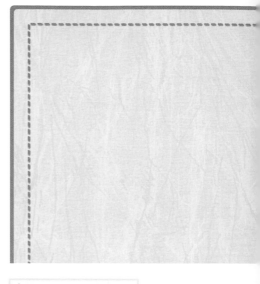

## STEP 1

*Trim the wadding back to fit the quilt top. Leave the backing fabric and quilt top fabric approximately 1 cm (½ in.) larger than the actual quilt top on all sides of the quilt. Fold the backing fabric inwards, and the quilt top fabrics inwards, so they both sit behind the wadding.*

> ◎ **TIP**
>
> Use this method if your quilt design does not need the addition of a binding.

## STEP 2

*Gently curve the corners. Pin the fabrics in place as you go.*

## STEP 3

*Make a quilting stitch just inside the folded edges of the quilt to secure the raw edges.*

# Separate fabric binding

Choose the binding fabric once all the quilt-making has been finished: it can make a calming or vibrant addition to a quilt at this stage, depending on what is needed.

## STEP 1

*Trim the quilt top fabric, backing fabric and wadding so all the quilt edges are even. Cut strips of binding fabric on the straight grain (if longer lengths are needed, join the strips on the diagonal).*

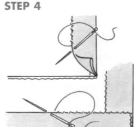

## STEP 2

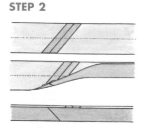

*Press all binding strips in half lengthways.*

## STEP 3

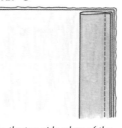

*On the two side edges of the quilt, place binding strips on top of the quilt top, matching raw edges, and stitch in place.*

## STEP 4

*Turn the folded edge of binding to the back of the quilt and slipstitch in place. Repeat step 3 on the other edges, leaving excess binding at each end of the quilt edge. Turn in this excess fabric when folding the binding to the back of the quilt, then stitch in place.*

# Mitred corners

A squared quilt corner can be mitred if a fabric print needs to continue around the corner. It is better to use one continuous strip of binding fabric here.

## STEP 1

*Trim the wadding, backing fabric and quilt top fabrics so all quilt edges are even. Begin in the centre of one side of the quilt, placing the raw edge of one side of the binding (right side down) against the raw edges of the quilt and folding in a small excess of fabric before beginning to stitch*

*the fabric layers together.*

## STEP 2

*Continue stitching until you reach the corner of the quilt, then stop stitching with the needle in the "down" position, a seam's length from the edge of the quilt. Pivot the work around the*

*needle and continue stitching along the next quilt edge.*

## STEP 3

*Continue stitching the binding until you reach the point where you began. Join the two ends neatly.*

## STEP 4

*Turn the opposite raw edge of binding fabric under and fold all binding to the back of the quilt. Slipstitch in place. Fold the corner tucks diagonally and slipstitch to neaten.*

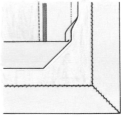

# Binding a curved quilt corner

If a separate binding fabric is required to continue around a curved quilt corner, cut the binding fabric strips on the bias to give them stretch and prevent the fabric puckering.

> **TIP**
>
> Curved corners can provide an attractive alternative to finishing a quilt and can enhance a curvilinear quilt design.

## STEP 1

*Trim the wadding, backing fabric and quilt top fabric so that all the quilt edges are even. Use a dinner plate or something similar to draw a large curve at the corners of the quilt; trim the fabrics back to this curve.*

## STEP 2

*Using one continuous strip of binding fabric and beginning halfway along one of the quilt edges, lay the binding right side down, raw edge to raw edge, on the quilt top and begin stitching in place, turning in a small amount of excess fabric to begin.*

## STEP 3

*Gently ease the stretchy, bias-cut fabric around the curve when you reach it. Finish the binding where it meets the point you began. Slipstitch to neaten. Fold the raw edge of the binding inwards and fold all the binding to the back of the quilt. Slipstitch in place.*

# Binding shaped quilt edges

Quilt edges can be shaped to follow the quilt top design or be cut freehand. To achieve a squared-off corner, use four separate bias-cut binding strips, one for each quilt edge.

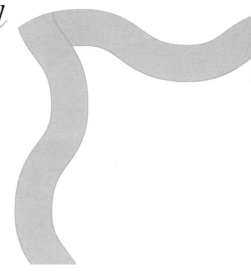

## STEP 1

*Trim the quilt edge, wadding and backing fabric to neaten the quilt edges and follow the shape required.*

> ### ⊚ TIP
> Cut fabric strips on the bias so they stretch and curve easily.

## STEP 2

*Fold the binding strips in half down their length. Working on two side edges of the quilt first, place the binding on the quilt top, raw edge to raw edge, and stitch in place, gently easing the binding fabric to follow the shape of the quilt edge. Turn the folded edges*

*of the binding to the back of the quilt and slipstitch in place. Repeat with the top and bottom edges, leaving excess fabric at either end of the quilt edge – this is turned in before folding the binding to the back.*

# Binding a scalloped edge

A scalloped quilt edge requires a continuous length of binding fabric that has been cut on the bias to allow it to stretch around the curves.

### STEP 1

*Mark the scalloped edge on the quilt top or follow the pattern of the quilt itself. Leave the wadding and backing fabric untrimmed until the binding has been sewn in place. Place the binding strip, right side down and raw edge to raw edge, on the quilt top. At each valley in the scalloped shape, make a small cut into the seam allowance of the binding fabric to help release any tension. Stitch the binding in place, keeping the needle in a "down" position when you pivot at each valley section. Continue until the binding meets the point where you started and fold in the two raw edges to neaten.*

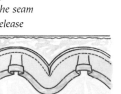

### STEP 2

*Trim the wadding and backing fabric so they are even with the quilt top. Fold the complete binding strip to the back of the quilt, helping the fabric tuck into a fold at each valley. Slipstitch the binding in place.*

> **TIP**
>
> Use an object such as a dinner plate to mark an even scalloped edge.

### STEP 3

*Neaten the fabric folds at each valley and carefully slipstitch the folds in place.*

# Folded-in handkerchief edge

A quilt with a pennant-shaped, handkerchief edge is difficult to add a binding to. The best way to finish it off is to fold in the two fabrics and not use a binding.

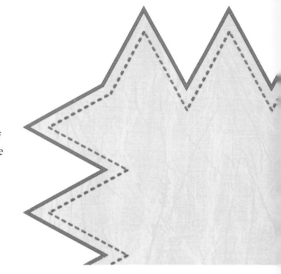

## STEP 1

*Trim the wadding, backing fabric and quilt top fabrics to the shape required, then trim the wadding to approximately 1 cm (½ in.) smaller than the two fabric edges.*

## STEP 2

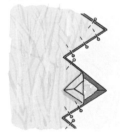

*Fold the backing fabric and the quilt top fabrics inwards evenly, pushing them behind the wadding. Pin in place as you go.*

## TIP

Alter the width or length of the spikes to fit in with the quilt measurements.

## STEP 3

*Stitch all the layers together with a quilting stitch made just inside the folded-in quilt edges.*

# Inset piping

Adding an inset fabric-covered piping can provide an attractive alternative to both binding and folding in a quilt edge.

### STEP 1

*Trim the wadding, backing fabric and quilt top fabric so each quilt edge is even. Cover the length of piping cord in bias-cut fabric and stitch*

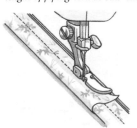

*the piping to the quilt backing fabric, neatening the point at which the two raw edges meet.*

> ### TIP
>
> The piping fabric can be a subtle colour that harmonizes with the quilt top, or a strongly contrasting colour.

### STEP 2

*Fold in the raw edges of the quilt backing so the piping is on the outside of the quilt and the raw edges are inside the quilt. Fold the raw edge of*

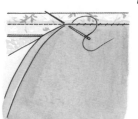

*the quilt top inwards evenly. Pin as you go along. Slipstitch the quilt top in place so it meets the inside edge of the piping and covers the row of stitching.*

# Inset sawtooth triangles

Adding sawtooth triangles to the folded-in edge of a quilt can give the illusion of a handkerchief edging without the need to shape the quilt itself.

## STEP 1

Trim the wadding, quilt top and backing fabric so all quilt edges are even. Trim the wadding so it is approximately 1 cm (½ in.) shorter than the quilt fabrics.

## STEP 4

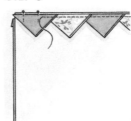

## STEP 3

Position these along the edge of the quilt backing fabric, ensuring that each triangle sits inside the previous one. Space the triangles evenly along the quilt edge, pin and stitch in place. Repeat on all sides of the quilt.

## STEP 2

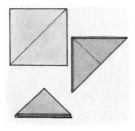

Cut and fold several sawtooth triangles of fabric.

Fold the backing fabric inwards, ensuring that the raw edges are inside the quilt and the triangles are sitting outside the quilt. Fold the quilt top fabrics inwards neatly, pin in place and slipstitch or secure with quilting stitches to finish.

# Inset prairie point triangles

Inset these triangles into a folded-in edge to add another dimension to a quilt. Try using a striped fabric, or scraps of different fabrics that have been used throughout the quilt.

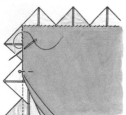

### STEP 1

*Trim the wadding, quilt top and backing fabric so all the quilt edges are even. Trim the*

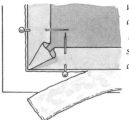

*wadding so it is approximately 1 cm (¹/₂ in.) shorter than the quilt fabrics.*

### STEP 4

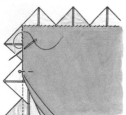

*Fold backing fabric inwards so that the triangles point outwards. Fold quilt top fabrics inwards. Pin and slipstitch to finish.*

### STEP 3

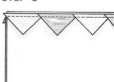

*Position these evenly on the right side of the backing fabric, matching raw edges. Pin and stitch in place.*

### STEP 2

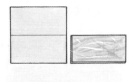

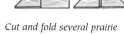

*Cut and fold several prairie point triangles.*

# Cleaning, Storage and Display

The aftercare and presentation of your quilt is important if it is expected to last and, hopefully, be passed down through the generations to follow.

## CLEANING

At some stage you'll have to think about cleaning your quilt. You need to consider the fabrics used in the quilt, including the wadding. Don't resort to professional dry-cleaning unless you are sure of the fibre content of the quilt and can discuss this with the dry-cleaners beforehand.

**Machine washing** If the quilt is quite robust – made from new, prewashed 100 per cent cotton fabrics, machine quilted and it contains a wadding such as polyester – you can launder it in a washing machine. Choose mild soap flakes rather than a detergent, and a cool wash setting. Tumble-dry the quilt afterwards, or lay it flat on a sheet to dry. Do not hang it on a clothes line – the weight of damp fabric and wadding could pull on the stitching.

**Delicate quilts** If a quilt is hand quilted, made from fragile or less robust fabrics (such as silks or pieces cut from old clothing), or if the content of fabrics and/or wadding is unknown, it is probably better to treat the quilt gently. Antique quilts or quilts with mixed and fragile fibres can be cleaned by covering the quilt with a length of calico or net and vacuuming through it, with the vacuum cleaner set to the lowest strength and held above the fabric fibres so that they are not sucked upwards.

## DOWEL

*There are several ways to display wall quilts: the most common method is to sew a tube of fabric to the top edge of the quilt, on the reverse side, where a length of dowel can be inserted. This is a requirement for exhibition quilts, but also means that the quilt can be displayed so that the dowel or hanging pole is not on show.*

**Washing by hand** If the quilt really does need a good but gentle wash, fill a bathtub with warm water and dissolve some mild soap flakes in it. Immerse the quilt in the water, gently pushing it downwards until the layers are soaked through. Knead very carefully to clean it. Leaving the quilt in the bath, let the soapy water drain away and refill the bath a couple of times with clean rinsing water. Once the water runs clear, empty the bath. Using a large sheet or towel, roll the wet quilt onto the sheet and lift it out of the bath. Lay the quilt out flat on top of the sheet, either on a suitable floor or outdoors on a warm day, to dry naturally.

## STORAGE

Be careful about where and how your quilt is stored. Buy plenty of acid-free tissue paper; if the quilt has to be folded, pad the folds with the tissue paper to avoid permanent creasing. Add more sheets of tissue between the layers and around the outside. Wrap the complete quilt in a cotton sheet or, if smaller, put it inside a pillowcase and store it away from direct sunlight and damp conditions.

## DISPLAY

If your quilt is to be displayed on a bed, make sure it is turned regularly. If direct sunlight shines in, turn the quilt face down so that it doesn't fade, or cover with an additional sheet to protect the fabrics.

Some quilts are intended to be displayed on a wall, either at home or in an exhibition. Again, try to avoid hanging the quilt in direct sunlight. Take it down at regular intervals and lay it flat for a few days to alleviate the stress on the fabrics and stitching.

## QUILT-HANGERS

*You can buy decorative quilt-hangers made from wire or wood, or just use a brass pole and some fancy cord, to make a feature of your quilt-hanging system. These can be used either with the tubular hanging sleeve, or you might like to add some hanging loops at the top of your project specifically for this purpose.*

# Glossary

**ACID-FREE TISSUE PAPER**
Used for storing textiles and quilts.

**APPLIQUÉ**
Attaching shapes and motifs of fabric to another fabric for surface embellishment.

**BACKING FABRIC**
A material used on the reverse side of a quilt.

**BEARDING**
The word used to describe the appearance of a fabric when a fluffy wadding has worked its way through the fibres of the fabric or emerged through the seams of patchwork.

**BETWEENS**
Specialist needles for hand quilting.

**BIAS-CUT FABRIC**
Fabric that is cut at an angle of approximately 45° to the straight grain and is very stretchy.

**BINDING**
Fabric added to the edge of a quilt to neaten it and hide the raw edges of all the layers.

**BODKIN**
A sewing needle with a blunt point and a large eye, for use with thick thread. It is used for corded quilting.

**BONDING WEB**
A web of adhesive presented in sheet form, which is used to glue two pieces of fabric together.

**CALICO OR CHEESECLOTH**
A very open-weave, lightweight cloth used as an interlining when working stuffed or corded quilting.

**COLOURFAST FABRIC**
Fabric where the dye does not run when it is immersed in water.

**CORDED QUILTING**
Also known as Italian quilting. A length of cord, yarn or wool is passed between two layers of fabric to provide dimensional interest to a quilted surface.

**COTTON**
Natural fibre, even-weave fabric or natural fibre thread.

**COUCHING**
Stitching down a length of thread, yarn or cord on a fabric for surface embellishment.

**ECHO QUILTING**
Stitching around a quilting design at a regular interval from the edge of the design to echo the design further.

**FRAME/HOOP**
A wooden or plastic structure used to support work that is being quilted or embroidered.

**HAND QUILTING**
Stitches that hold the layers of a quilt together and are sewn by hand.

**INSERTION STITCHES**
Decorative stitches sewn as a means of joining two neatened edges of fabric together.

**INTERFACING**
A stabilizing fabric that is ironed or sewn to the reverse side of a material that requires support.

**ITALIAN QUILTING**
Also known as corded quilting. A length of cord, yarn or wool is passed between two layers of fabric to provide dimensional interest to a quilted surface.

**KANTHA QUILTING**
A style of quilting originating in Bangladesh, which consists of running stitches in coloured threads.

**LIGHTBOX**
An illuminated box that allows designs to be traced onto fabric with ease.

MACHINE QUILTING
Stitching that holds the layers of a quilt together and is sewn on a sewing machine.

METALLICS
Fabrics or thread that contain a man-made fibre with a high-gloss sheen.

MITRED CORNERS
Corners that have been folded and sewn at an angle of 45°.

MUSLIN
An even-weave fabric with a homespun appearance. Cream or bleached white in colour.

PATCHWORK
Patches of fabric that have been joined together to form a pattern.

PIECING
The sewing together of patchwork shapes.

POLYESTER
A man-made synthetic fibre used in fabric, threads and wadding.

POUNCING
Transferring a design onto fabric through holes in paper using a cloth filled with powder or chalk.

QUILT
Two layers of fabric with padding in between, stitched together. Commonly used as a bed covering.

QUILTING
Utility and/or decorative stitching that holds the three layers of a quilt together.

ROTARY CUTTING EQUIPMENT
A safety mat, a safety ruler and a cutting wheel with a sharp blade.

SASHIKO
A style of quilting originating in Japan, which is usually stitched in designs based on a grid.

STABILIZING FABRIC
A fabric that is ironed on or sewn to the reverse side of a material that requires additional support. In quilt-making, usually a nonwoven interfacing.

STRAIGHT GRAIN
The fibres that run across the width, or down the length, of a piece of fabric.

TACKING
A large, temporary stitch, used to hold layers of fabric together. In quilting, used to secure layers of fabric (or fabric and wadding) together prior to quilting.

TEMPLATE
A shape used for making patches to be used for patchwork or appliqué, or a motif for a quilting design.

TRAPUNTO
A form of quilting where areas of the design are padded with stuffing.

WADDING
A material used for padding or insulation. In quilt-making it is used to fill the area between layers of fabric to provide surface relief.

WALKING/EVEN-FEED FOOT
A sewing machine foot that is used to help ensure that the top and bottom fabrics in a quilt are fed through the machine at the same speed.

WATER-SOLUBLE PEN
A fabric-marking tool with ink that is removable in cold water.

WHOLECLOTH QUILT
A quilt where the top is made using a whole length of fabric, rather than being pieced together.

# Further reading

## EMBROIDERY

Barnden, B. *The Embroidery Stitch Bible* (KP books, 2003)
Eaton, J. *Mary Thomas's Dictionary of Embroidery Stitches* (Trafalgar Square Publishing, 1998)
Harlow, E. *The Anchor Book of Free-Style Embroidery Stitches* (David & Charles Publishers, 1997)

## QUILTS AND QUILTING

Donaldson, J. *Add-A-Line: Continuous Quilting Patterns* (American Quilter's Society, 2002)
Eddy, C. *Quilting Basics* (Barron's Educational Series, 2003)
Finley, R. *Old Patchwork Quilts and the Women Who Made Them* (Charles T. Branford, 1971)
Gaudynski, D. *Guide to Machine Quilting* (American Quilter's Society, 2002)
Jenkins, S. and Seward, L. *The American Quilt Story* (Rodale, 1992)
Poe, A. *Quilting School* (Reader's Digest, 2003)
Sandbach, K. *Show Me How To Create Quilting Designs* (C & T Publishing, 2004)
Seward, L. *The Complete Book of Patchwork, Quilting and Appliqué* (Mitchell Beazley, 1997)
Tinkler, N. *The Essential Sampler Quilt* (Teamwork Craftbooks, 2005)
Tinkler, N. *Quilting With A Difference* (Traplet Publications, 2002)

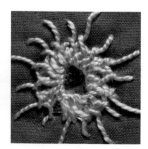

# Suppliers

**UK SUPPLIERS**

COATS CRAFTS
PO Box 22
Lingfield House
McMullen Road
Darlington, County Durham DL1 1YQ
Tel: 0044 (0)1325 394237
Email: consumer.ccuk@coats.com
Web site: www.coats.crafts.co.uk

CREATIVE GRIDS (UK) LTD.
Unit 4, Swannington Road
Broughton Astley
Leicester LE9 6TU
Tel: 0044 (0)845 450 7722/7733
Email: sales@creativegrids.com
Web site: www.creativegrids.com

THE COTTON PATCH
1285 Stratford Road
Hall Green, Birmingham B28 9AJ
Tel: 0044 (0)121 7022840
Email: mailorder@cottonpatch.net
Web site: www.cottonpatch.net

THE QUILT ROOM
20 West Street
Dorking, Surrey RH4 1BL
Shop: 0044 (0)1306 740739
Mail order: 0044 (0)1306 877307
Web site: www.quiltroom.co.uk

WHALEYS (BRADFORD) LTD
Harris Court
Great Horton, Bradford
West Yorkshire, BD7 4EQ
Tel: 0044 (0)1274 576718

Email: info@whaleys-bradford.ltd.uk
Web site: www.whaleys-bradford.ltd.uk

SEW CREATIVE
Wroxham Barns
Tunstead Road
Hoveton, Norfolk NR12 8QU
Tel: 01603 781665
Email:
sewcreative@sylvia79.fsbusiness.co.uk

PATCHWORK CORNER
51 Belswains Lane
Hemel Hempstead, Herts HP3 9PW
Tel: 01442 259000
E-mail: jenny@patchworkcorner.co.uk
Web site: www.patchworkcorner.co.uk

# Index

# Picture Credits

Quarto would like to thank Nikki Tinkler for supplying the photographs that appear on page 6, 7 (top left), 9 and 247.

All other photographs and illustrations are the copyright of Quarto Publishing plc.

While every effort has been made to credit contributors, Quarto would like to apologize should there have been any omissions or errors – and would be pleased to make the appropriate correction for future editions of the book.

# Author Acknowledgements

I would like to thank all my family for their support and encouragement, and also Liz Pasfield and Penny Cobb at Quarto for their input and advice. Thanks also to Classic Cottons, Coats Crafts UK, Whaley's of Bradford, The Quilt Room and The Cotton Patch for generously supplying many of the fabrics and threads used in the book.

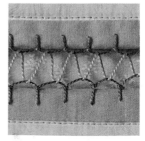